A THOUSAND TEARS: AN ENABLER'S JOURNEY

Angie G. Meadows, RN, MSN
Perry Meadows, MD., JD
Sarah J. Meadows, BS

Abstract

Identifying the Enabler's Cycle and our conflict with individuals caught in addiction. Identifying a manipulator, devourer or toxic relationships in our life and learning to confront and detach. This book is a useful tool in understanding our dysfunctional patterns when our loved ones have Substance Use Disorder. It also includes multiple self-assessment tools: Enabler's paradigm, entanglement gauge, anxiety quotient, trust scales, and much more.

A Thousand Tears, LLC
PO Box 561
Lewisburg, PA 17837
enablersjourney@gmail.com
www.enablersjourney.com
Angie G Meadows Youtube.com
Rock of Recovery podcast

Contents

PREFACE

This book gives no advice. It only gives information for observation and self-reflection and allows the ability to set aside the confusion and make rational decisions based upon what is best for you. The content is a compilation of our healing journey from a lifetime of observing addiction behaviors.

This book is also not about losing hope or giving up hope. It is about our journey to escape from the Enabler's Cycle, which allows one to then view the situation objectively and clearly. The cycle will lead to your own destruction if you do not escape. Only when you remove yourself from the cycle will you be able to objectively assess all options for your loved one with **Substance Use Disorder (SUD)** and attempt to assist them on the road to recovery.

The main writer is Angela. My constant coaches and editors are Perry and Sarah. When going through this journey and hanging onto an imaginative dream of future success for our loved one, we were going financially deeper and deeper in debt. We realized the definition of "insanity" according to Alcoholic Anonymous is to continue to do the same thing over and over again and expect different results. We had no choice but to stop or drown financially. We had to seek our own recovery from people and circumstances we could not control or change. Watching our loved ones suffer with addiction and enabling, we had no power to make a difference. At times, it was unbearable torture.

This book will help you identify the dysfunction in relationships and assist in stopping destructive enabling behaviors. Additional research is needed to add with this book to further assist your loved ones who are minors with addiction issues or those involved in life-threatening overdoses.

Consider all this information and use your best judgment to determine what works for you. Only you can identify what does or does not apply to your circumstances.

I use he/him to refer to the person with addictive behaviors. You may use whatever gender pronoun applies to your situation.

I use the words Substance Use Disorder (SUD) to refer to our loved ones caught in any addictive behavior. This could include the strongest street drugs, prescription medications, excessive use of alcohol, gambling, pornography, gaming, food addictions and a myriad of other things that may control our lives. This is not meant to be a negative term, but an inclusive term to refer to those with dysfunctional coping skills. This includes us and our addictive enabling behaviors.

Although this book is based upon our experience with people with substance use disorder, the principles also apply to those in domestic violence and with other addictive behaviors.

INTRODUCTION

Though we cry a thousand tears today, tomorrow we could cry a thousand more and still have no power to change the life of our loved one in addiction. The chaos and disorder of addiction is devastating. It doesn't matter if our loved one is functional in society (hiding the addictive behaviors), or if our loved one has catastrophic and dysfunctional behaviors living between the streets, homeless shelters, and prison with frequent life-threatening overdoses. There is no safety or peace for them or for the family.

I hear your cries for help. After searching for answers for over two decades, I can assure you ... there is only one answer for the enabler. We must **stop controlling and manipulating people and circumstances!** This behavior causes our suffering. We must seek counseling and recovery for ourselves. It is vital to understand the role we play in this masquerade. There will be no peace or safety unless we pursue recovery for ourselves with strong, healthy boundaries, support groups, and counseling.

Enablers are also addicted. We are addicted to the drama and rescuing our loved ones with addiction behaviors. Our suffering is intense and enabling gives us a reprieve from suffering. The enabling places us in denial and gives us an allusion of righting what is wrong. Then, we become overbearing finding someone else to blame as we pardon the person with SUD from any responsibility for their actions.

We, as enablers, know destruction is near and we seek to prevent the sorrow of consequences for our helpless loved one. Yet, the very relationship we seek to save is being destroyed by our irresponsible excuse making and manipulating of outcomes. **Every time we choose to interrupt the harsh**

consequences of addictive behaviors, we only drive them deeper into the grip of the disease of addiction to ruin the possibility of recovery.

The hearts of enablers are full of goodness and kindness. Their motives are to assure safety and a prosperous future for loved ones. These characteristics make us easy targets for smooth-talking persons with SUD and can lead to catastrophic financial ruin. We must learn to steer clear of this destructive path.

I am ready for peace. I am ready for a safe environment. I am ready to stop grinding my teeth and pacing the floor at night. I am ready to stop walking in fear. I want to stop and mend **my broken heart**. How can I do this? I seek mental, emotional, and physical health for myself. I educate myself on addiction behaviors and my corresponding responses which continue to incapacitate and prevent me from enjoying my life and future. If you are ready to get off this roller coaster and pursue **your** recovery, follow me. We will forge this path together.

DIAGNOSIS OF THE PROBLEM

CHAPTER 1: IDENTIFYING THE DYSFUNCTION

The realization that I was addicted to my adult loved one with SUD set me on the path of recovery.

"He's not sick, you are," said the woman at Al-Anon. Proceeding to defend my mental soundness with a horde of reasons, I described how I was the responsible one and not the "sick one". Smugly she responded, "Well, who keeps allowing the insanity to continue by interrupting the consequences."

Stunned at the realization that I was the "sick one", I implored her to speak to me about how any loving mother could reject involvement in their **adult child's** life. Particularly a momma who could foresee all the future ramifications of taking such a stance against his addiction: financial devastation, unemployment, destruction of his health, loss of his home, divorce, abandoned and aborted children, imprisonment, and certain death if he continued on this path.

She assured me all these consequences were looming possibilities. The consequences were more imminent with my excusing his irresponsible behaviors. Setting firm boundaries and not allowing myself to succumb to the emotional manipulation, was the only sane thing to do.

In my last weeping plea to her, I said, "Mothers don't turn their backs on their children." Quickly she retorted, "Yes, but those mothers don't have to deal with this garbage! We have to get tough and stop being part of the problem."

It has been a 28-year journey of analyzing my behaviors and the behaviors of others around me and documenting my observations.

> My decisions are not based on manipulation from an out of control individual!

Detaching emotionally has been a developmental survival skill I have had to learn and re-learn again and again.

> Detachment has allowed my decision making to be based upon what is right for me.

Eventually, I was able to let go of insanity and recover my own heart. Giving myself permission to move forward, I can now enjoy my own life. I can care for others in the wake of the person with SUD's destructiveness and bring healing to those who want help. I can release my loved one to the consequences of his own choices and hope that he will soon want to stop his suffering and find recovery. Let us begin…

THE ROAD OF ACCEPTANCE LEADS TO PEACE:

The Stages of Enabling of an Adult with SUD

An enabler is one who empowers another to persist in self-destructive behaviors, such as substance abuse, by providing excuses or by making it possible to avoid the consequences of such behavior. (Merriam-Webster, Inc. 2018) An enabler must realize they are not dealing with their rational loved one, but with one driven by the insatiable demon of addiction.

> The only way to recover your loved one from this bondage is to recover yourself first.

Elizabeth Kubler-Ross, in her work "On Death and Dying" identified the five stages of grief: 1. Denial 2. Anger 3. Bargaining 4. Depression and 5. Acceptance

As with grief upon the death of a loved one, enablers must go through the same stages to obtain freedom from the mental torment associated with enabling another adult with irresponsible addictive behaviors.

Denial

Whenever an enabler makes excuses, covers up, or accepts the financial consequences of another person's behaviors, it literally places them in denial. Soon, another crisis surfaces. The enabler must then decide whether to accept the situation or attempt to "fix it" and return to their denial. During this stage, one frequently reacts with shock, which results from an awareness of possible impending death due to the serious destructive behaviors of a loved one. Unfortunately, it is not a shock that might bring about change, but one where the enabler asks, "What will the other people think?" Or "I need to help him, and he will appreciate it so much, he won't do it again." The enabler will often assist their loved one in the diversion of blame and escaping consequences.

Anger

Once an enabler has made a financial investment in helping their loved one, they become angry when the person with SUD is ungrateful and not making steps to change. The anger is particularly intense if he starts stealing from them and continues lying to them. If there is no anger, the enabler is truly deceived, thinking their continual righteous acts of goodness will cover the unrighteous ones made by the one they are protecting. The enabler can be a soft target if they have unresolved guilt from the past.

Bargaining

During this stage, the enabler becomes a manipulator for "good outcomes". But, a manipulator just the same and will begin preying on the good will of others, including friends and family, to "help" the individual in addiction. The manipulation by the enabler may involve lying or even threats to obtain assistance for their loved one. Then, the coercion extends to the person with SUD. This is a masterful skill to extort good behavior from their loved one with addiction behaviors. Manipulation is then learned and perfected by the person with SUD; it is flipped back onto the enabler and used to fuel our exaggerated guilt to continue financial extortion.

Depression

When reality sets in and the enabler realizes they are not the one who can save their loved one and cannot manage another person's morality or actions, despair sets in. The enabler sinks into confusion and guilt. They think they are being too harsh and rush to save their protégé to alleviate the depression. This continues the toxic relationship. In this stage, they have fallen into a repeating cycle of bewilderment, feeling helpless and hopeless. The tendency is to throw money at it and revert to the **stage of denial** and sweep the problems under the rug. **It is impossible to cure addiction issues with money.** Instead, you have received their financial consequences and they are free from responsibility. Now, their only care is the next high.

Acceptance

It is not until the enabler comes to an end of their coercing and realizes things are broken and beyond "their" control that they can find acceptance.

The enabler is powerless to change another and must let go of the responsibility to do so.

9

This is followed by an extensively painful mourning period, which feels like an awfully long funeral dirge. In this process, the enabler must die to their own wishes and plans for their loved one. This "emotional death" gives the enabler the freedom to live their life and invest themselves in others who can be safely loved and enjoy healthy relationships.

> When an enabler matures and develops healthy boundaries, their loved one may also desire recovery.

The enabler must emotionally release the one they cannot save from his/her own compulsions. This is done by allowing them to experience the pain of their own consequences.

> Enablers do not need to stay on the path of destruction with their loved one with SUD.

As a recovering enabler, do the research and give them addresses and phone numbers for substance disorder treatment centers, medication-assisted treatment clinics, halfway houses, food pantries, homeless shelters, and support groups. However, **the enabler must leave the decision of recovery in their loved one's hands.** Even a functional person with SUD with a home, car, and employment must be fully responsible for their financial obligations. Allowing them to wallow in the pigpen of consequences might wake them up to the reality of the future they are destroying and become a catalyst for change.

So, my fellow enablers, could this mean death of our loved one? Absolutely! Addictions can certainly lead to death.

> The enabler must realize their over-responsibility is fostering their loved one's under-responsibility.

Let the person with SUD learn responsibility for their actions quickly while they are young. Let them bear the brunt of full responsibility for their legal and financial issues. When they experience very painful circumstances, they may choose to change. **If you rescue, the next consequence of your loved one's actions will most likely be more destructive and maybe even life threatening.**

> The road of an enabler is mental torment and despair.
> The road of acceptance leads to peace.

This book will begin to assist us to explore the toxic behaviors of a person with Substance Use Disorder and our corresponding dysfunctional behaviors. Until we can clearly see the game the addictive substances drive our loved ones to play, we cannot break the cycles of enabling.

ADDICTIVE AND ENABLING BEHAVIORS

Addictive Behaviors	Enabling Behaviors
Manipulation	Merciful/Tender-hearted
Lying	Fixer
Stealing	Over-responsible
Cheating	People pleaser
Blaming	Desires good outcomes
Coercing	Manipulates for good
Hiding/Cowardly	Assist loved one's in
Obsessive thinking	addictive behaviors:
Compulsive/Impulsive	Blaming
Negative thinking	Making Bail
Grumbling/Complaining	Motivated by guilt
Pretending helplessness	Gullible
Immature	Philosophy is to keep
Raging	picking them up until they can
Bullying	stand.
Anger	Believes money can fix the
Abusive	problem.
Irresponsible	Believes consequences are
Crisis making	unfair or harsh.
Diverting the attention	Fearful
elsewhere	Anxious and Stressed
Separating enablers from	Denies the addiction is real
others	Feels no one loves the
Gossip/slanders anyone	person with SUD but them
who opposes them	Thinks they are their loved
Isolating	one's savior
Peer dependent	Thinks if they fix the

temporary consequence
one more time, the
addiction behaviors will stop.
Denial
Excuse maker

CHAPTER 2: COURAGE TO STOP THE ENABLING

When you disengage from the chaos of toxic
relationships, you will be considered the enemy.

Courage is the strength to do the right thing in the face of opposition and internal fears. It is difficult to be misjudged and labeled as the problem when you are the responsible one. The challenge to reclaim your life and maintain your sanity comes when you refuse to rescue others from the consequences of poor behaviors. The root of enabling is the desire to alleviate the suffering of others.

- The whole family may dive in and enable the loved one with SUD. Expect to be accused of being uncaring and cold hearted. You are only valuable if you can be used or manipulated.
- The person with SUD may slander and destroy your character, exaggerate your past failures and flip the meaning of your words.
- It becomes gut wrenching to watch the lunacy, the lies, the manipulation, the confusion of impending squandering of life savings of elderly enablers, or your future inheritance.
- It is like watching a train wreck that cannot be stopped.

> At this point, your anxiety will match the level of involvement you continue to have with the individual with SUD and the other toxic enablers.

- Even if you have no verbal contact, your anxiety may still be very high. In order to decrease and stop the anxiety, you must emotionally detach.

(See chapter 19 "Detachment")

- If there are elderly or unsuspecting honest people being consistently conned, we might keep some contact with them to speak truth and be the voice of reason.
- You must stay emotionally detached and **never ever give them cash**: the person with SUD or other actively enabling enablers.
- If you enable an enabler and pay their bills, you have just enabled them to continue enabling their loved one without any consequences of their own.
- It may take a decade for the prime enabler to be completely bankrupt and lose everything, but this is the path they are choosing.
- Do not pay off loans for prime enablers or they will have good credit and get more loans.
- If an elderly enabler is now frail or having signs of dementia, and you choose to take them into your home, a **"No contact"** rule must be in place between them and the person with SUD.
- Formerly honest enablers may lose their senses and rob other family members and friends. They may, also, turn a blind eye when the person with SUD steals.
- Do not loan an enabler money for their bills if they have not repaid what they previously borrowed from you.
- You must understand most enablers are as addicted to enabling as their loved one is to their substance of choice. It is the enabler's way of attempting to "control" outcomes.
- The rescuing has become their identity and enablers live in pseudo-reality.
- The enabler's toxic relationship with their loved one with SUD is an unhealthy love. Enablers are persistent to keep up the appearance of normalcy.
- Even if they see the lies and manipulation, they may choose to cover it up or continue excusing it.

- The level of forgiveness given, without any restitution or accountability, is amazing.
- They are sacrificing for their loved one and feel it is a noble cause.
- The enabler cannot coddle or bribe their loved one with SUD into changing.
- Unfortunately, the enabler and the person with SUD both need tough consequences.
- It is difficult to legally prove an enabler with early signs of dementia is being abused. If they have freely given money away to this loved one in the previous decade, it is especially difficult to prove they are not acting out of "free will". They may be having hundreds of dollars a day embezzled. The person with SUD soon preys on the memory loss and uses the same excuse for the need of money in the evening as they used in the morning.
- It may be appropriate with the elderly in early dementia to attempt to contact elder abuse or an attorney to get control over the estate and finances. Hopefully, our laws will change, and we will be able to place their money in a trust where there will be money left to care for them in case of illness.
- This is a devastating and depressing end for 70-80-year-old.
- We need to have the legal power to contact the credit bureau or the elderly will be conned into taking out loans on everything and eventually be unable to meet their payments and lose everything.
- If the money is gone by the 2nd or 3rd of every month, instruct the enabler where the food pantries are located.
- If they give their car to a person with SUD, let them ride a bus or save money for a taxi. Only give them a ride if it is convenient and is something you would have normally done.
- The sooner an enabler loses everything, and their credit is ruined, the sooner they will be forced to stop.
- Don't get things out of the pawn shop or you will need to do it every month.

If you do retrieve an item out of the pawn shop, keep control over it.
- Sometimes, all you can do is prepare your heart for a destitute parent, grandparent, or sibling.
- If there is domestic violence, child abuse, neglect, or endangerment, seek further counsel.

FOR YOURSELF

- Get yourself healthy. Go to support groups and counseling.
- Learn exceptionally good boundaries.
- Learn to say "NO" with kindness and strong firmness.
- If the elderly or other enablers become destitute, you can decide how or how not to intervene. Sometimes you have to let them go on Medicaid and to a nursing home or they will bring the chaos in your home and will continue their enabling by giving all their pension or Social Security check away and expecting you to care for them financially and physically. I give you permission to say "no" and place conditions on your finances and on your physical availability to care for them.
- If you take an enabler in your home, they must be accountable to you for their money or find another place to live.
- Sometimes, the elderly enabler with mild-moderate dementia needs to be hidden from the person with SUD.
- If there are no enablers, you may have an opportunity to intervene with your loved one with SUD and arrange for confinement in prison to sober up and then into rehabilitation.
- If this doesn't work, you may need to leave your loved one in the streets and attempt to intervene to provide rehabilitation opportunity about once a month, until he is done with the streets and ready to do the

work of recovery. This is extremely dangerous and needs to be a last resort with hard-core addiction behaviors. A safer option would be to work with the authorities to incarcerate your loved one until he is ready to work a recovery plan.

- The cost of stopping your participation in this lunacy may be relationships with other family members. Stand firm! If you can get one or two loved ones to stop enabling, the others may learn quicker.
- At the very least, you can have your life back. Turn your focus onto children, friends or other loved ones who have been neglected.

PROFILE

Now, I want to profile the players. If you can see what you are dealing with logically, you will be less likely hooked into the emotions of the game.

Person with active SUD: The Con

- Con-man game
  - o Nice
  - o Sweet
  - o Pleasant
  - o Helpless, etc.

If you say no, or call them out on their emotionally manipulative kindness, the con man plays the victim and you are the abuser. Soon, they create havoc and you are cut out of the triangle with emotional/relationship suicide. They will even convince their other enablers you are crazy. After all, you are between them and their next high. This can be dangerous and even life threatening for you and can escalate quickly. Get out of the way!

Person with active SUD's: Character when confronted

- Bully
- Belligerent
- Argumentative
- Thief
- Slanderer, etc.

Most likely this person cannot receive help until they are confined in prison (without an enabler bailing them out, making excuses, and hiring an attorney). This event could turn out to be the stimulus they need to propel them into recovery program with court accountability. It could save their life.

Protect your identity or it could be stolen as payback.

Prime Enabler

- Obsessed with their loved one with SUD and how to rescue them from consequences of poor choices
- Passive/aggressive
- Manipulative with person with SUD as well as their co-enablers
- Can praise or rail their co-enablers based upon their enabling assistance
- Bribing for good behavior
- Blaming everyone for the person with SUD's problems
- Lying and yet believes every lie their loved one communicates to them, even if they know it to be a lie
- Very sneaky and secretive financially
- Very unstable boundaries
- Trust in money to fix problems

- May truly desire to stop enabling, but they are relationally controlled

Enablers will keep others on the hook to help enable the loved one with SUD. These are relationships where the enabler uses and abuses others to benefit their loved one. They claim they are being abused by you when your enabling stops. When the enabler is bankrupt, they may blame a spouse or prey on other innocent family members until others are also bankrupt. Blaming others is becoming a honed skill. Prime enablers are masters at playing the victim.

This person's life is characterized by cyclical confusion and denial of the root issues. Love them from a distance with your head and not your heart or you may be drawn into the game repeatedly. This enabler cuts off anyone they can't use to help enable their loved one. They may be completely convinced what they are doing is wrong and swear they will never do it again. But they have no backbone. To recover, they must take steps to receive help and to be accountable financially to people they trust to make right decisions for them.

CO-ENABLERS

Primary Co-Enabler

This unhealthy relationship allows the prime enabler (spouse, parent, stepparent, grandparent, adult child, sibling, domestic partner, etc.) to play the victim with others in the family by claiming some of the other co-enablers are greedy, controlling and don't love the person with SUD and won't care for their needs. (Albeit, the financial support is going for drugs and the primary co-enabler is usually very aware of this scenario.)

The primary enabler and primary co-enabler have great conflict. This sets the stage for sympathetic enablers to feel sympathy towards the enabler.

The co-enabler may also have addiction issues. They can be functional and able to work or manage finances. Often, they will escalate conflict, so they have an excuse to use their substance of choice. Usually this is a socially acceptable substance like prescription pills or alcohol.

> They usually don't see their own issues but focus on the person with SUD as being the main problem.

Passive/Aggressive Primary Co-enablers

- Can be very responsible at times and then very irresponsible.
- Can perpetuate multiple conflicts with the person with SUD and the primary enabler. This may give them an excuse to drink or use excessive prescription medications if they have addictive issues.
- May have substance use problems, if so, the guilt usually drives them to appease the primary enabler by giving financially to cover the cost of enabling.
- Often, they love the primary enabler very much and assist in enabling to keep the peace and to show support.
- When they realize the gravity of the impending financial doom, they can rant obsessively.
- The relationship with the primary enabler is so out of balance that it could escalate to domestic violence or even homicide.
- Can also pretend to wholeheartedly enable the person with SUD, but the motive could be out of malice to attempt to finance their "accidental" overdose.
- Are relationally dependent and not strong enough to walk away.

Sympathetic Enabler

- Believe everything the primary enabler says.
- Defends the primary enabler.
- Takes pity on the primary enabler, because the primary enabler plays like they are abused and used. They may have distressful financial consequences. The primary enabler is compelled to rescue and assume responsibility for the loved one caught in addiction and the sympathetic enabler frequently does not seem to understand the depth of this behavior.
- Tries to keep up with the primary enabler's doctor and dental bills.
- May even make sure their wants are supplied: eating out, hair dye, and other comfort items.
- May buy flowers and little gifts to comfort the primary enabler and cheer them up. The primary enabler has convinced them that they are a victim of bad luck or poor circumstances, not their own dysfunctional enabling choices.

The primary enabler is believable because he/she is telling what they think is truth, but their reality is skewed by their loved one's lies and manipulation. Primary enablers are deceived and deceive the sympathetic enabler.

> The primary enabler sets up an offense between other co-enablers and sympathetic enablers and anyone who won't play the game.

This diverts the attention from the main issue and causes chaos and confusion. The primary enabler emotionally manipulates co-enablers and the sympathetic enabler for money just like the person with SUD manipulates them. They justify this by thinking their loved one with SUD will recover, and it will be worth any sacrifice. The hard luck stories are worthy of a Hollywood movie. The sympathetic enablers do great harm.

> The primary enabler is never confronted and challenged to admit their dysfunctional behaviors.

All the focus is on the problems of the person with SUD or on the conflict with other co-enablers. If you discuss the primary enabler's dysfunctional behaviors and equitable consequences, they are quick to defend and blame anyone except the primary enabler.

Entangled Enabler

- Is one who has completely ceased to participate in enabling activities but is still relationally connected with the prime enabler.
- Needs to be aware that the primary enabler and person with SUD may plot to ruin their reputation and finances.
- If you choose to stay, prepare yourself.
- They may:
    - Call the police and falsify or exaggerate domestic violence reports
    - Hurt themselves and say you did it
    - Rob your financial accounts
    - Steal your car
    - Pawn your multi-generational coin collection and tools and then blame you
    - Give away all your belonging to flea market dealer for a couple hundred dollars
    - Sell your $2,000 electronics for $100 while you are out of town
    - Act sweet one moment and be a snake to you the next
    - Accuse you of abusing them when you are confronting them about their dysfunctional behaviors
    - Blame you for their loved one's problems

o   Poison your food/drink

> If an entangled enabler stays to protect the primary enabler from a person with SUD, he/she is relationally dependent in a dysfunctional way.

The entangled enabler may have a fear of being alone, need to be needed or be deluded into thinking he can control the situation if he stays. The primary enabler will be aggressive and bullying if the entangled enabler doesn't respond with sympathy to their loved one with SUD. Consider the possibility that the entangled enabler needs protection from the primary enabler and the person with SUD.

If you are an entangled enabler and you choose to stay, disconnect emotionally and make decisions based upon what is best for you. Go to support group meetings and counseling to help unravel the confusion and to receive support for your decisions.

Detached Enabler

- Continues to support other co-enablers.
- Is emotionally detached from the person with SUD and the primary enabler and is recovering.
- Has begun practicing healthy boundaries and developing healthy relationships.
- Usually has been an enabler and has done several years of recovery work.
- Sees the issues and the dysfunction clearly.
- Motive for staying connected to co-enablers is to assist them in recovery.

Caution

If you stay involved with other co-enablers who refuse to disentangle from toxic relationships physically, financially, and/or emotionally, you will continue to experience emotional trauma which may harm your recovery. Also, if other co-enablers disrespect your boundaries, this will interrupt your recovery.

The more involved the detached enabler is:

- The more likely they will become a blame target for the person with SUD's circumstances and consequences.
- The more likely they are to become entangled again.
- The less likely they will be able to develop healthy relationships.

The primary enabler is obsessed with their loved one with SUD.

Unsuspecting Co-Enablers

This is to **WARN** <u>Unsuspecting Co-enablers</u> about the behaviors of a **Primary Enabler:**

- **Doctors** – to convince them of his need for pain meds.
- **Lawyers** – to convince them of the injustice done for minor work injuries, slip and falls, minor car wrecks, or poor outcomes of medical procedures. Primary Enabler will hire lawyers to convince the court their loved one with SUD is innocent of criminal charges. Primary Enabler assist in filing for worker's compensation benefits and later disability benefits.
- **Insurance companies** – to falsify testimony for the car wrecked the previous night.
- **Police** – to falsify reports on the co-enablers that are hindering the enabling.

- **Probation officers** – to convince them of his outstanding improvement and his lack of need for accountability.
- **Child support authorities** – to insist his whereabouts are unknown.
- **Court authorities** – primary enabler will intervene on warrants and claim to be a guardian and make payments and do without their own needs being met. They will post bail.
- **Magistrates and Judges** – to convince them that he fulfilled his nine-month rehabilitation program in four months. She will show up in court as his representative.
- **Employees** – to give false references for him. They will call him off work.
- **Banks** – to cover all bad check charges and false deposit ATM claims.
- **Credit card companies** – to insist their identity was stolen again and they don't know who could be doing this.
- **Neighbors** – to coerce in giving them daily transportation.
- **Sunday school friends** – to go to their homes at midnight and borrow "emergency" money.
- **Benevolence fund from the church** – to say he is dying and needs money for treatment.
- All potential **new lovers** are reeled in quickly with affirmation and adoration from the primary enabler. It is hopeful that a new enabler will arise, and the primary enabler can have a break.

Conclusion

If the primary enabler is providing for the person with SUD, don't provide for them. If you live with a primary enabler and/or a person with SUD, it will be a war zone. There is no recovery if there is no accountability for past or future enabling behaviors. These are painful relationships to be in or even to watch from a distance.

THE ENABLER PARADIGM

The whole addiction process falls apart without a primary enabler.

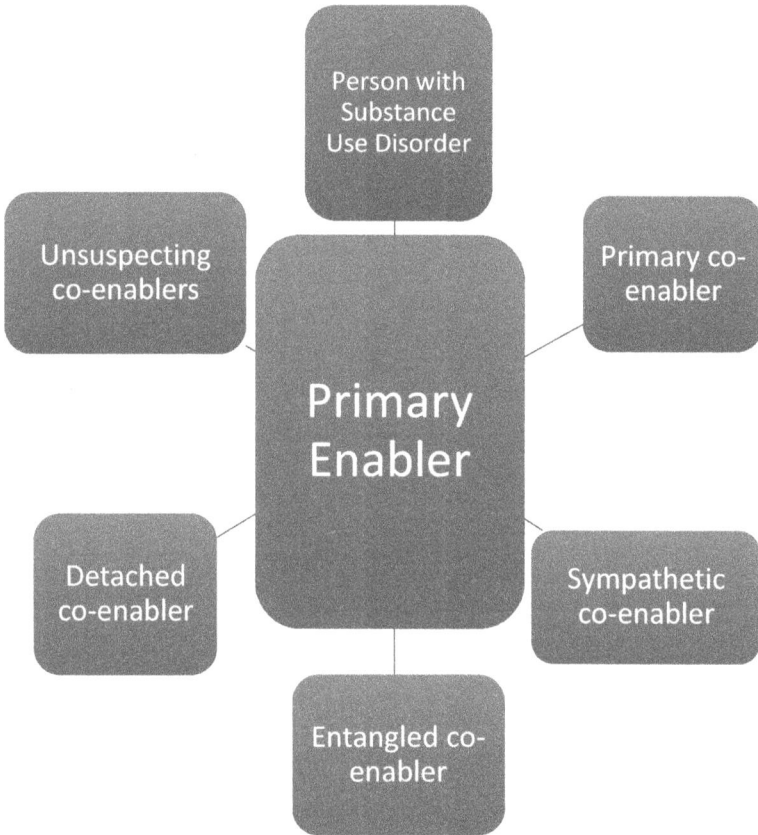

Person with Substance Use Disorder

Unsuspecting co-enablers

Primary co-enabler

Primary Enabler

Detached co-enabler

Sympathetic co-enabler

Entangled co-enabler

CHAPTER 3: TEN TYPES OF ADDICTION

*Addictions not only cause suffering; addictions are
birthed from festering unresolved emotional wounds.*

Next, let us evaluate the extent of the problem: Addictions not only cause suffering, addictions are often birthed from festering unresolved emotional wounds. We can ask forgiveness for our part in causing wounds and be an example by working on our own recovery.

These next ten levels of addiction are the ones I have personally observed. As you read them, evaluate which level of unhealthy behaviors you and your loved one's exhibit. Then, you will be able to understand the level of dysfunction wherein you are contending.

Hard-core Addiction

Driven by impulse and lack of self-control

This person with Substance Use Disorder will lie, cheat, steal from every employer, friend, or family member. They may rob and bankrupt their elderly grandparents or make fraudulent worker's compensation claims. Others cut, stab, and burn themselves to manipulate ER doctors for pain medications. They may steal the identity of other friends and family for credit card fraud. Previously, they have robbed employers and lack dependability and are now unemployable. It is not unusual for them to have abandoned children and beaten mates in their past. Often, they have a long criminal history and started drugs at an early age. They are extremely stubborn and difficult to help. They have paranoia and can be unpredictable with others who stand between them and drugs. These individuals with SUD are master manipulators. (See "Manipulation" Chapter 13) They can be innocent and helpless with someone one moment, then fraudulently embezzle money raging and bullying with a gun or a knife the next. They are extremely dangerous.

This person's ancestors usually have a long history of addiction issues. They may also have a co-morbidity with other behavioral health issues. They may have been neglected or abandoned by their father and/or mother, and raised by a single-parent, grandparent or someone else. Childhood sexual abuse is common. They are greatly lacking in self-control and are driven by impulse and emotions. They may be violently angry or grandiose with narcissistic traits. They may have many self-destructive behaviors such as cutting, illicit sex, or other high-risk behaviors. They are frequently IV users and there is no drug they will not chase. Usually, they only slow down when they feel the full effect of severe consequences. As soon as they become comfortable (fed, clothed, warm, and dry), they can find no self-control to be sober. Our loved one with SUD may want to stop but has no power to do so. This hard-core person with SUD needs to be incarcerated to protect others and to be protected from themselves. Then, they may be willing to work a recovery program in lieu of a prison term to explore the deep wounds that drives them to self-destruction.

Functional Addiction

Driven by guilt and shame

This person is fainthearted and lacks maturity or needs emotional healing from past trauma. They can be veterans who cannot reconcile war as a righteous act. They drink to medicate their conscious. They may have had an abortion and are struggling to forgive themselves for this or something else in their past. They could be stuck in a mourning stage over the death of a loved one or a bad divorce. Vacillating between blaming themselves and blaming others is common. They can usually maintain employment but have very poor coping skills and struggle in relationships. Keeping up appearances becomes more important than admitting they need help.

Overwhelmed Fainthearted

Driven by fear of failure

They lack confidence, feel inferior and isolate themselves. They often are hard workers and others take advantage of them. Their addiction keeps them from healthy relationships. Frequently, they whine and feel helpless or are loud, obnoxious, and verbally abusive. They can be very depressed. This gives them an excuse to shut down real life and go into addiction behaviors to cope. They cycle into abusing others and being abused by others.

History of severe childhood abuse

Driven by emotional immaturity

They are numbing the pain. Physically, sexually, emotionally abused, or neglected and abandoned children can grow up to have chronic physical and emotional pain. They are difficult to treat because the root issues need time to surface and are hidden by a myriad of social issues that takes precedence.

Codependent/Enabler

Driven by a desire to "save" or "fix" others.

This person finds his/her identity in helping others. They also have the philosophy that if you just keep picking up an individual, they will eventually stand. They are attempting to help by sacrificing themselves and their financial stability for the "love" of another. This is an immature sick love. (See "Love" chapter 16) They can be passive/aggressive when they feel like doormats. Eventually, this "over responsibility" for another makes them destitute and a burden on others. Frequently, they lose the very relationship they sought to save. They do not understand addiction issues and think they can fix what is broken in their loved one by rescuing them from consequences. They often "enable" to stop the emotional pain they feel for their loved one or their social embarrassment over the situation. They also think more money can "fix" any problem. If this person gets free from an abusive relationship and doesn't diligently work a recovery program for themselves, they will unknowingly hook into another abusive relationship attempting to resolve their past in the present. They end up with different people, different names and faces, but the exact same scenarios of abuse.

Leech/Sponge

Driven by lack of morals and laziness

This person seems to be the party animal. They look for financially stable people to attach themselves to and then work their "magic charm" to become entangled financially or emotionally with him/her by marriage, having a child together, or a business deal. Once they have them entangled, they dominate and control by emotions, manipulation, confusion, chaos, blaming and an assortment of lies and pseudo-reality.

Dry Drunk or workaholic

Driven by exaggerated, immature, unstable emotions

These individuals with addictive behaviors find their identity in their reputation and in their work ethic. They may be recovering from addiction and have not dealt with their emotional issues. They could be reputable professionals who work 16-18 hours a day. They have difficulty saying no to themselves and are frequently frustrated. They can be tyrants and oppress others especially children, mates or co-workers. **They can be addicted to raging, bullying or complaining.** These behaviors give them an allure of power and seems to temporarily release the pent up unresolved emotional pain of the past. They have many behaviors of a person with SUD: **blaming, coercing, manipulating, bargaining, denial.** Since they are not prone to numbing their emotions with mind altering substances, they have lots of energy to work themselves up into a fretful frenzy. They can be prone to beat and batter their enablers physically or emotionally. There is a tendency for them to be control freaks and feel very empty and lonely and have trust issues. Yet, they erroneously see themselves as healthy individuals because of their accomplishments or their bank account. They might also struggle with varying degrees of behavioral health issues.

Helpless dependency addiction

Driven by inner fears and brokenness

This person may have a chronic illness, car accident or a work injury. They may hate pain medication but are caught in a pain cycle. They are unable to cope with the withdrawal to stop the prescription medications. They need emotional stability and other alternatives to relieve the pain. They usually have a great need to learn boundaries and to nurture and care for themselves.

Dual Addictions: Sub-Addictions can run simultaneously with dominate addictions.

Entertainment Addiction

Driven by peer pressure, self-consciousness

This person attaches to food, games, computers, phones, television shows or actors and binges when they feel lonely or overwhelmed. They also struggle feeling connected or give their loyalty to the wrong people. They may be fearful of connection and avoid eye contact during conversation by watching their phones while their mates, children, family, or friends attempt to engage them. They are inordinately afraid to move forward, even in safe environments. Often procrastination and complacency keep this person from achieving the goals they desire to accomplish. This person has not accomplished a solid identity. They have difficulty saying no and lack the confidence to establish healthy boundaries. Their insecurities lead to physical illnesses and psychosomatic pain syndromes. Some of this seems the norm in the teens and early 20's, but this is not a stage you would want to be stuck in.

Love and Sex Addiction

Driven by lack of self-control or attachment disorders

This person connects through sexual intimacy. They have weak impulse control and/or are addicted to the hunt and the rush of a new partner. They do not know how to love or become intimate in a relationship to bring about the emotional fulfillment they truly desire. They often are drawn to emotionally unavailable people. They were not affirmed as a child or may have been over indulged. They may have been orphans or in foster care. Even if their family unit was intact, their identity was most likely not established; therefore, they attach to sensual indulgences. They may have developed a habit of fantasy thinking or indulged pornography early in life to escape reality. Their need to satisfy their cravings is higher than their need to be responsible in their behaviors towards others. They have great difficulty being quiet or alone. They may have difficulty sleeping at night.

Conclusions

Individuals with addiction cannot identify the root issue(s) and are moody, broody and depressive and are attempting to medicate themselves instead of learning healthy coping skills. **Self-pity and negative thinking mental loops** are common and racing thoughts can reign supreme. Yet some loved ones with SUD have no cognitive thinking but attempt to micro-manage their lives by controlling every temporal thing in their environment. Others may be extremely careless and throw all caution to the wind and live recklessly.

Most individuals in addiction live a life characterized by the imbalance of **undisciplined thinking and exaggerated immature emotions resulting in self-destructive behaviors.** This keeps them in an emotional whirlwind and dominates every area of their lives and leaves them feeling empty.

> Those in addiction suffer from an identity crisis and can identify with anyone who appears to be happy or having fun. These are pseudo-relationships.

The younger a person engages in addiction behaviors as a coping skill, the more stunted their emotional development. A seventy-year old man can still be throwing fits like a four-year old. A thirty-year old who started drugs at the age of twelve may still developmentally be a young adolescent.

This is a sampling of the different addictions I have observed. I am certain there are many more. Many of these levels of addictions overlap. The more addictions identified in our lives; the more unraveling that needs to be done.

> Addictions make our relationships and home environments unstable. The instability of addiction diverts our attention from the root issues and fuels our perpetual suffering.

Recovery will achieve great momentum when the answers become visibly achievable and when we can separate healthy and unhealthy behaviors clearly. The bulk of this process takes 1-2 years. When we find community, hold each other accountable and teach it to others, our recovery becomes more stable.

> Have no delusions, this is work.

CHAPTER 4: SELF-EVALUATION

Until we can evaluate our losses and our gains we cannot understand where we have been and the work needed to arrive at where we want to go.

IDENTIFYING THE SET UP

What were the circumstances from childhood or early adulthood that could be the root causes for addictive behaviors and/or dysfunctional coping skills? I would like for you to name all the destructive influences of your childhood. Add any other circumstances not listed that may have caused you a wound.	
Identify Childhood Set up:	Yes/no
Domestic Violence	
Abandoned	
Neglected	
Brain Washed	
Incest/Rape or other sexual abuse	

Enabling parent	
Verbally abusive parent/sibling	
Alcoholic in the home	
Substance use disorder	
Severe street drug use	
Homeless	
Divorce	
Unable to please parents	
Not validated	
Not safe	
Unable to feel comforted/loved	
Promiscuous parent	
Parental marital conflict	
Single Parent	
No parent	
Emotionally absent parent	
Incarcerated parent	
Abusive siblings	
Bullying peers	
Given drugs or alcohol at a young age	
Other:	
2) What are the outcomes you can identify from your emotional childhood pain? It is important to understand the consequences of this negativity. Add any insight to your list. **Outcome:**	

Confusion	
Fear	
Anxiety	
Stubbornness	
Rebellion	
Misplaced values	
Poor decision maker	
Habitual liar	
Negative thinking or racing thoughts	
Exaggerated emotions	
Unforgiving/bitterness	
Irresponsible	
Mental Confusion	
Mental Torment	
Fantasy escape (addictive thinking)	
Depression	
Enabler (over responsible)	
No moral compass	
Passive/aggressive behaviors	
Addictive behaviors (could be as simple as food compulsions)	
Self-mutilation (cutting)	
Self-destructive (alcohol/drugs/speeding/gambling)	
Promiscuity	
High-risk behaviors	
Other:	
3) What good things did you have as a child?	

Let's make a positive shift and find the good things to dwell on and develop an attitude of gratitude.	
Childhood Comforts:	
Nice Friend	
Friendly personality	
Pets that I loved	
I wanted to do right	
Intelligent	
Good with my hands/crafty	
Hobbies	
Athletic	
Musically inclined	
Loving grandparent	
Stable adult influence	
Food	
Shelter	
Home	
Kind teacher	
Other:	
4) Who did you identify most with as a child? It is good to evaluate the people you admired. They have helped you build your identity. For example, have you practiced dysfunctional behaviors like one of your parents? This may have been an attempt to	

identify with them to win their approval.	
Peers	
Absent Parent or abusive/enabling parent	
Older sibling	
Sports hero	
Historical hero	
Cult/gang leader	
Musician	
Do you identify with healthy or unhealthy individuals?	
Did you identify with those you were trying to please?	
Did you identify with one who was emotionally unavailable to you?	
Did you lead or follow a crowd?	

You could also evaluate your current relationships: marriage, children, employer, etc. Examine any dysfunction in your life. Focus on the good. Establish some future goals for improvement within your control. **Now, reshape your future to look different from your past.**

GROUND ZERO

CHAPTER 5: WOUNDED HEART

Recovering ourselves from a wounded heart, is a simple shift in our thinking.

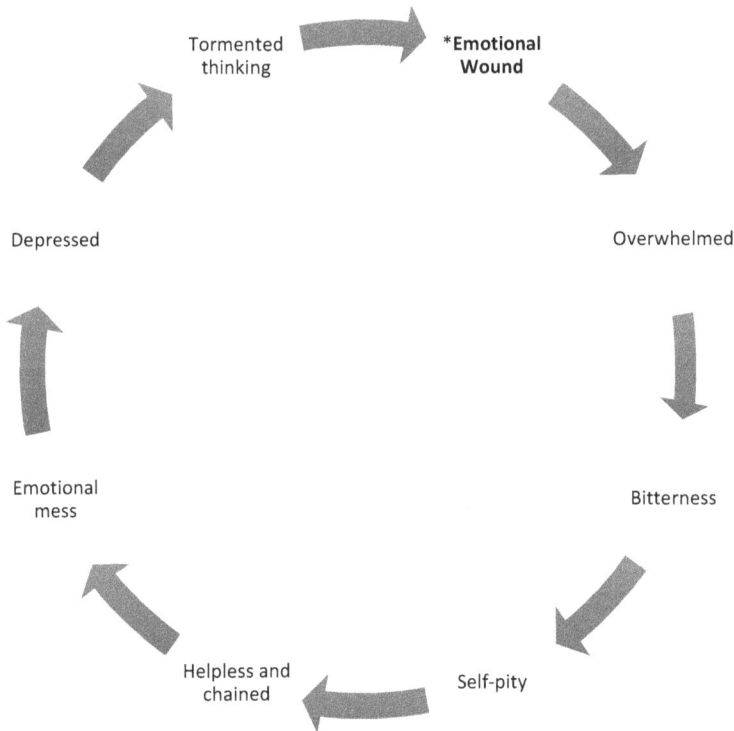

Tormented thinking → *Emotional Wound

Overwhelmed

Bitterness

Self-pity

Helpless and chained

Emotional mess

Depressed

First, we are going to evaluate what caused our wounds. Next, we will analyze each developing stage of a festering wound. We will identify how to change from being emotionally ruled and explore how to take control of our lives by detaching from people and emotions that are not safe.

> Recovering ourselves from a wounded heart, is a simple shift in our thinking.

It is not easy, but simple. Discovering our wounds and facing them can feel like a turbulent sea, you may need a support person to explore this with you. Don't give up! Our recovery from a wounded heart comes next!

Identifying your Wounded Heart

1) Unresolved Emotional Wounds - Until we **identify the wound or the guilt that drives the self-destructive enabling patterns of thinking and behaviors**, it is going to be difficult to find lasting peace.

> Self-destructive enabling patterns: Attempting to control another adult's behaviors and their consequences or circumstances of their poor choices, as if, it was my responsibility.

This behavior causes us a wound. It could be as simple as someone disappointing us and not taking us on a childhood fishing trip. Or the wound could be growing up in domestic violence, parents with addictive behaviors, incest, rape, and decades of chaos.

It is when we take control over our lives and say, "no more" that the healing can begin. First, I must admit there is an imbalance and a need to heal. This step brings to light the wound(s) which hold me back. In this phase, it is helpful to dialogue with myself through journaling. During these reflective moments, I am free to say and feel all my feelings and thoughts.

List all my wounds (guilt). Are they in the past, current, or ongoing?

List unsafe people and environments. Are they in the past, current, or ongoing?

Which people need firm boundaries? Which ones do I need to avoid altogether? List the semi-safe people who you can visit for short periods of time after emotionally detaching from them. List the people who make you crazy and need to be avoided.

Semi-safe people

Crazy makers

I love lists. They help me see black and white. When I can identify my crazy makers by their past behaviors and lies, I can set up boundaries, so I am not sucked into the game again. If you do not feel free to write, journal this dialogue in your head so you can visualize what is going on in your life by stepping back from the emotions and chaos and discover the facts.

> Wounds keep me emotionally immature.

When I know the facts, it breaks the confusion and its emotional control over me. Facts give me **mental thinking direction** which can separate me from my cycle of chaos and negativity and help me **reclaim my own identity**. It can give me permission to take control of my thoughts. Otherwise, people and circumstances dictate what I think and feel. That needs to stop!

Processing my thoughts through reflective thinking develops the realization that these emotions may be intensely exaggerated. If the abuse is active or if my abuser flips behaviors and pretends to be safe, I need the facts to empower me to protest by exercising my "No" muscle and distancing myself from the abuse.

Is there a safe place inside of me?

When I trust myself to choose healthy thoughts, actions, reactions and relationships, I feel safe. I will be able to process emotions and change them. For example, if I do not feel loved, I find a quiet place within myself and breathe deeply and say: "I am loved". During this exercise, I recall the people in my life who are safe and those who do love me. Then, I intentionally purpose to let go of the toxic relationships and pursue healthy people and environments.

Maybe there are no safe people in my circle of life. I get that! But that doesn't mean I have to stay stuck in a cycle where I continue to loath myself. I can start with me!

I can learn to be a safe person for myself. No longer will I tolerate negative thinking or berating from myself or others. Instead, I can learn to meticulously identify my emotions and feel them but then set them outside of me (See "Is my pain inside or out?" Chapter 8). In this exercise, I give myself permission to enjoy my day.

What does my daily self-talk say to me?

Whose voice is in my head?

Do I wake up anxious or worrying?

Is my sleep restless?

Do I have worry insomnia?

As I separate my identity from loved ones with dysfunctional behaviors, I can develop my own identity. I can know who I am and determine how much I will and will not tolerate. If I am stuck in domestic violence, I can empower myself by developing a plan of escape. I always have choices. I may not like them, but I have choices. Sometimes, it is Yucky choice #1 or Yuckier choice #2.

Can I identify the lies I believe about my circumstances?

Can I identify the lies I believe about myself?

Now I need to be on a quest to find safe support groups, healthy people or children that desperately need nurtured and protected. I can shift from being responsible for another adult's dysfunctional behaviors AND the consequences of those behaviors. Right now, I can be responsible for my own thoughts, feelings, and behaviors.

2) Overwhelmed - A thought or feeling that overpowers me with grief, fear, guilt or shame.

> Enablers have been well trained by their abusers to not trust themselves to make a right decision or to be strong enough to stick with it.

What emotion is overwhelming?

What thoughts or circumstances are fearful?

What causes anxiety?

What makes me angry?

Was there one traumatic event that began my imbalance and made me feel overwhelmed?

What mental response happens when I am overwhelmed?

- **Do I have anxiety attacks?**

- **Do I stay in bed?**

- **Do I get moody and withdrawn?**

- **Do I start fantasy thinking/daydreaming attempting to escape reality?**

- **What does my self-talk say when circumstances are beyond my control?**

Negative talk from yourself or others can be a quick slide into destructive habits or irresponsible actions. It is like your heart faints and it shuts down and says, "I don't care!"

| Negative talk from yourself or others hits the "sabotage" button.

If we can identify the destructive thinking, we can interrupt the behaviors that follow by changing our thinking. If I can start recognizing the cycle of my abuser's building agitation or my noxious ramblings as defective, I can go to my support group or seek help immediately to stop the spiral of my destructive coping skills (fighting back physically or verbally, uncontrollable crying, over eating, destructive substance use, recklessness, cutting, isolation, depression, sexually acting out, etc.) Now, I can choose to do something different this time.

3) Bitterness - marked by intensity and severity of physical and emotional suffering.

Personally, I can feel my bitterness. Literally, I can feel my physical response to it. My jaw clenches, I grind my teeth and start getting snippy and fuss at others who are innocent in the situation. **My abuser isn't usually safe to confront.** Then my stomach churns and I develop restlessness and I can't sleep soundly.

> Unnecessary harshness from me causes more bitter responses from others.

This can make me shut down to my environment and take the pain inside of myself and my suffering intensifies and can even paralyze me from making healthy decisions.

Identify what kinds of things/circumstances make you feel bitter?

This is easy to do. Listen to your complaints. Whatever you are grumbling about is what has made you bitter?

We must learn to process this bitterness and push it outside of us and not identify with it or it will eat us up from the inside out.

What kind of bitterness is in my life? Example: Domestic violence, controlling spouse, parents, or boss, smooth talking deceptive persons with SUD, irritating co-worker, emotionally unavailable mate, etc.

What kinds of things do I do that increases bitter circumstances in my life? Example: Manipulation, stubbornness, cursing, defiance against authority, frequent conflicts, complaining, arguing, lying, manipulating, gossiping, slandering, brooding or acting moody.

4) Self-pity - a self-indulgent musing on my own misfortunes, suffering, and sorrows.

When I first started identifying my self-pity, I was shocked at how much of it I indulged. The focus in my life was on the empty or destructive relationships and my resulting unmet needs. This would position me in a tailspin and bring up a legion of past wounds I had not resolved. This was a self-comforting behavior. Compassion or affirmation was greatly lacking from others in my life. So, **brooding, and self- pity had become my dysfunctional friends.** This response to my circumstances made me stagnant and perpetually immature.

> Just for the fun of it, take one day and count the times you indulge self-pity, sulking, pouting, whining, and withdrawing.

5) Helpless and chained - defenseless and without support. Recognition of this stage is easy. It can be characterized by isolation, curled up in my bed, paralyzed to trust others, binging on comfort food, television, shopping, calling off work, sexual fantasies, etc. These behaviors tend to slow the racing thoughts of anxiety and helplessness. Our racing thoughts can spiral on a negative loop and keep us anxious. Others may have no cognitive thoughts, only primal exaggerated emotions with an intense anger, grumpiness, or brooding.

What things or circumstances make you feel helpless?

6) Emotional Mess – No peace in my life. There is a continual dread of impending doom or death of a loved one. In this stage of carrying my wound alone, I go through the motions but enjoy nothing.

What problem is your peace hiding behind?

7) Depression. This phase seems inevitable with a loved one who is abusive and/or caught in addiction. This is the place where we realize this vicious cycle of depravity will never end for us, we feel stuck. This phase feels like death. There is great mourning.

What disturbances are you experiencing that are characteristic of depression? Problems: sleeping, loss of appetite, binge eating, isolation, crying, anxiety, memory loss or poor concentration, racing thoughts, or just plain emotionally numb.

8) Tormented – Obsessing and completely losing our identity. If not corrected, this can lead to chronic stress and chronic health issues. It can also lead to mental breakdown and suicidal thinking or taking excessive prescription medications attempting to cope.

I know I am in this phase when there is a perpetual conversation in my head with abusive or addicted loved ones. Waking up in the middle of the night trying to rationalize or talk some sense to them, is very common. "If I could just say the right thing, they would stop these behaviors!"

Is every thought focused on helping another "stop" their addiction/abusive behaviors?

Am I attempting to control the circumstances to prevent the next grump, growl or verbal explosion?

Is there intense fear when the phone rings or the doorbell chimes? Is it them? Am I going to have to face their wrath if I say "no"? Are they in jail again? Have they overdosed again? Are they dead? Who have they hurt now? Am I in danger? How can I hide? What should I do?

How many conversations do you have daily with yourself or another about the situation?

Can you talk about anything else?

When your mind is idle can you think about anything else?

What do your idle thoughts say?

Where negativity has been planted, we can expect thorny branches and rotten fruit.

Whew! We must unravel this mess!

CHAPTER 6: RECOVERY FROM A WOUNDED HEART

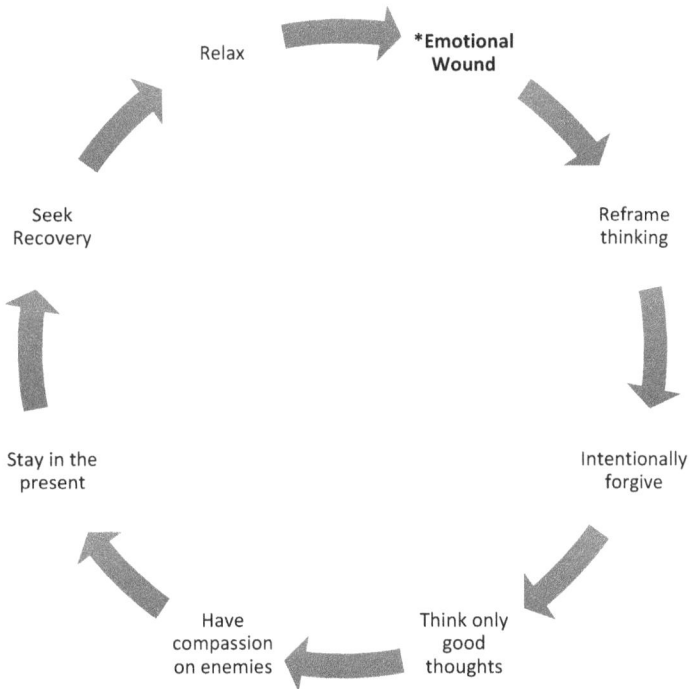

Relax → *Emotional Wound

Seek Recovery

Reframe thinking

Stay in the present

Intentionally forgive

Have compassion on enemies

Think only good thoughts

Be patient with yourself. It takes time to conquer poor habits of undisciplined thinking.

It is vital that we recognize our wounds and seek restorative healing. The goal is to come to a place of acceptance and peace. Then, we can make plans for future independence and to remove ourselves from the people and places that keep us in chaos. One of the greatest skills I have learned is how to deal with my exaggerated emotions. Controlling my foolish emotions and the destructive negative thinking cycle is a skill that must be cultivated. We cannot be guided by our emotions. We must have the truth of right thinking to direct our path. In this chapter, we will discuss some ways to heal from our wounds and set our feet firmly on solid ground.

Foolish emotions, if indulged, take over my life.

Recovery from Emotional Wound

Do not take a wound inside of yourself, but instead use it as a spring board for growth.

1) Emotional Wound. This is the same wound as in the "Wounded Heart Cycle," but today, we will "own" our self and take back our identity and respond with mental intelligence and not with emotions.

What would your life look like if you rejected this wound as if it never happened?

2) Reframe your thinking with truth. Name your suffering. State the facts.

What is the truth?

Who is or was your offender?

Is there anything you could have done differently to stop or correct the situation?

3) Purpose to forgive. Forgiveness is an act of your will, not your emotions. Forgiveness does not mean trusting this person again. Nor does it mean making myself available to be abused. It is a conscience and repeated choice to forgive every time I sense bitterness. Eventually, my emotions will follow, and I will have no animosity for my past abuser. Forgiveness sets me free. **If I am currently being abused, it is not time to forgive.** It is time to exercise my power and boldly say "NO!" and plan to disentangle and distance myself from this unsafe person.

Who do you need to disentangle or distance yourself from?

Whom do you need to forgive?

To whom do I need to make amends? When irritated, I used to verbally mistreat store clerks or waiters/waitresses with harshness. It was not until I purposed to return and apologize that I stopped. The inconvenience and embarrassment of going back and accepting responsibility for my unkindness empowered me to break this bad habit. I only had to do it three times and I was free from this rotten behavior.

4) Think only good thoughts. Declare war on negative, self-defeating thoughts! This takes purposeful planning. I have to focus on good mottos such as: "I am loved. I am healthy. I am strong and stable." I speak things over myself that are not true as if they were true. This lets me see myself differently and empowers me to change.

Name two negative things you say to yourself. Now change the words. For example:

"I can't do anything right." vs. "I can do

whatever needs done and if I fail, try again."

"I mess up everything." vs. "I can be patient with myself."

"You will never amount to anything." vs. "I can make a plan and be kind to myself and learn from any failure."

"I am unlovable." vs. "I can learn to love myself."

Negative statements are a quick slide to destructive thinking.

Make certain to **stay in the present and enjoy every precious moment.**

Do not ruminate in the past or stress over the future. Sometimes, there is a need to go back and analyze, learn and heal from the past and make a structured plan for future goals. Support and accountability partners are needed for progressive growth.

Learn to put every thought through this thought test. This takes work. This takes an awareness of my thoughts and feelings and then inventorying my past to see where they started. Follow the breadcrumbs and discern where the lies in your head originated. Then dispel the lie with the truth.

Are your thoughts...

Honest and true? vs. Lies and half-truths?

Fair and good? vs. Dishonest and bad?

Lovely and pure? vs. Ugly and mean?

Good report? vs. Gossiping?

Praising and positive? vs. Slanderous and negative?

Write down recurring idle thoughts. Are they true?

I receive whatever I give!!! It is the principle of **sowing and reaping**. If I plant corn, I won't grow green beans. If I plant negative thoughts or words, I will reap a multitude of negativity.

Negativity manifests itself in my life as anxiety and fear.

How does negative thinking manifest in your life?

One kernel can produce a hundred kernels of corn. Could one negative action, deed or thought reap a hundred like it? Likewise, could one kind and hopeful thought or response reap a hundred more positive interactions? Even as I establish boundaries with abusive or unsafe people, I can always be patient, kind and very, very firm. I can distance myself. I can hide myself. I can be quiet and refuse to escalate the problem. I can walk away.

5) Have compassion on your enemies. This breaks their tormenting power over your thought life. This is something I do whether I feel like it or not. This is for me, not for them. I can practice compassion when I am safe. When I can see people for who they are, I can have realistic goals for our relationship. This propels me forward in my recovery. (See "Love" Chapter 16 to identify healthy love.)

Keep a short list of offenses done to you and offenses you have done. Review the list every evening and ask forgiveness or forgive. I can do this with another person or on my own. This can be done through journaling. It's a simple act which can free me from carrying the burdens of the day. If the burden comes up again, I can remind myself to let it go again. Tomorrow, I can start with a clean slate!

Caution

1)   Do not go back to ask forgiveness when it would set you up for more abuse.

2)   Do not assume responsibility for the outcomes of someone else's poor choices.

3) Do not go back when it would open old wounds for the other person or make things worse.

4) Do not go back and expect the other person to own their offenses and repent to you.

In these situations, I go to my accountability partner and obtain good counsel and confess to them.

Insight

There are people in my life who are unstable. They are sweet and kind one moment and savage and raging the next. These types of people can hold us hostage by getting us to believe they truly have a good heart and it is only the circumstances (or me) that causes them to explode and rage. As a matter of fact, they profess repeatedly and very loudly about their good deeds. Hmmm! Really? Well, here is the truth. **There are some dysfunctional relationships that hold us captive because we want to believe the best.**

We may be dealing with three different people in one:
1) The first person is the one they pretend to be.
2) The second person is the one we think they could be.
3) Take off the mask and you will find the real person: raging, abusive, argumentative, manipulative, selfish, lying, unkind. (Need I go on?)

Permission: Give yourself permission to do whatever it takes to protect yourself from such stupidity. These are toxic relationships that need to end or at the very least have lots of distance. **When people act like enemies, love them from afar.**

If your enemy is beating you (mentally, physically, emotionally, or financially), you will not be able to heal. It is your responsibility to STOP the

cycle!!!

6) Stay in the present. How do I do this? I refuse worry, fretting or anxiety, and I place my full attention on whatever task is at hand. **Just because nonsense entered my head does not mean I have to entertain it.** I can use my willpower to kick it out and replace it with something worthwhile. Listening to pleasant music while I do dishes or clean is refreshing. Learning something new can stop the negative ruminating. It is hard to fret while I am studying Spanish words or practicing an instrument to play in a community orchestra.

Insight

There are some problems or repetitive thoughts that go on for decades. It's like going around and around the same block just with different scenarios. The conclusion is the same: I am helpless to change the situation. This could be an injustice in the present or past you cannot reconcile. It could be a wayward adult child who is devastating their lives with substance use. We can think of these things all day and night, but **there is no way to solve the unsolvable.** We cannot think our way through the problem or around it or past it and more rumination of the situation just **robs us of today**. There are some issues that are bigger than me and I cannot fix them, no matter how hard I try. If you are dealing with an adult who ends up in the same trap financially month after month, your financial rescuing is only crippling them. They will not assume responsibility for their own behaviors, finances, relationships, or employment outcomes until you step back and confidently give them their own problems to solve. Say to them, "I have complete faith in you. You are smart enough to figure this out."

7) Seek your recovery. There are a few things you can do:
A) Evaluate your part in the problem. You can only be responsible for

yourself, not other adults.

B) Educate yourself on your responsibility to not enable, rescue and make allowances for immature, irresponsible or abusive adults.

C) Seek deliverance from the person(s) abusing or taking advantage of you. Set firm boundaries. Empower yourself.

D) Find safe people and places to build community, support groups and/or professional counseling.

E) Develop other interests: gardening, woodworking, crafting, photography, music, art...

F) Find ways to invest in yourself.

8) Relax. Take a deep breath and let go. **Mental relaxation is a maturity skill** that needs to be cultivated and practiced through doing what is right for yourself first. This is literally not worrying about another person's problems. This may sound selfish. It is selfish in other circumstances, but not when you are being abused or entangled with one in addiction. You cannot trust an irresponsible people to make decisions for you. You must think of yourself and consider your future stability.

One caught in addiction only thinks as far as their next high. They are not concerned about you being comfortable, having a savings, retirement or even a place to call home. So, if stability in life is valuable to you along with comfort, warmth, savings, retirement, home, paying your bills, etc., it is mandatory to plan for your finances **not** to be manipulated and extorted from you by an adult lover, child or grandchild pretending to be helpless. **A person with SUD can become a master extortionist.**

Insight

When we exercise our "No" muscle or when we hold others accountable for their actions, they may abuse us even more. Be prepared and have enough independence established to protect yourself. **Those caught in**

addiction as well as other enablers are experts at manipulation. (See "Manipulation" Chapter 13) Also, when you refuse to financially enable irresponsibility or destructive substance use, expect more abuse and expect **relationship suicide. They will purposely destroy the relationship and even make it your fault.** If you aren't prepared, it can be devastating. (See chapter 19 on "Detachment".)

Who can I help?

The ones who:

- want help finding a rehabilitation center
- will respect boundaries
- appreciate my doing the right thing. Then I can give them the names and phone number of rehabilitation centers, day programs, AA, NA, Celebrate Recovery meetings, anger management programs, counselor's names, etc. **Until they are ready to assume full responsibility for their actions, they are beyond my help.**

PEACE

When you are actively in recovery, the confusion and chaos in your life will start to subside. Then you can begin to enjoy your life.

If you just said, "I can't have peace until they are in recovery." You are way too entangled with another adult and their problems. If you are mourning and being over-responsible for their problems, they don't have to change and can keep running down the wrong road dragging you with them. It may be time to kick them out of the nest and let them find their wings.

How can you strive for peace in your life today?

CHAPTER 7: TRUE AND FALSE RECOVERY

- Unless you can identify the difference between true and false recovery, it is impossible to know if the loved one you are enabling is beginning to recover.

As you recover from enabling and your loved one begins recovery from SUD, strong boundaries and distance in the relationship is most likely necessary.

TRUE & FALSE RECOVERY CHART

Broken heart... grieving over their losses	Sorry for consequences, not behavior
Paying back anything stolen	Lots of emotions, crying, anger, mood swings
Setting boundaries to prevent themselves from falling back into old habits	Good behavior (temporarily) to make up for wrongs
Setting up	Self-destructive

accountability partners	thinking/behaviors
Being open and accountable in every area of life	Saying "I am sorry." No plan to change.
Confessing past wrongs (with trusted person) Plan for restitution.	Makes excuses (hiding full truth/blaming others)
Seeking help	Trying to weasel out of consequences
Sticking to a plan developed by counselor or authority	Refusing to talk over issues. "No one tells me what to do." Demands blind trust.
Walking daily in recovery.	Playing a good game, while secretly engaging in addiction behaviors.
Serving others without a desire for reward or a motive to manipulate others	Justifying self and grandiose thinking. They only do chores or favors with a motive to manipulate for selfish gain.
Placing structure in life. Make bed, take out trash, fold laundry, do the dishes, etc.	Avoids responsibility.
Schedule (work)	Embezzles money and cons elderly or weak for

	money. Misuses money allotted.
Earns trust one day at a time	Escalates emotions to cast confusion
Looks for a reason for past failures and working through past wounds to find healing	Creates crisis and diversion. (Self-destructive behaviors.) Runs away. Cuts self. Threatens suicide.
Finds healthy social settings	Returns to dysfunctional friends
Works towards developing boundaries to establish a safe environment	Resents submitting to authority
Corrects self by confessing and asks for forgiveness often.	Double talks
Speaks truth even if there are consequences	Lies
Accepts responsibility for actions	Blames
Provides for self and pays what has been borrowed and begins to care for their children or elderly parents.	Selfish, bullies, dominates, plays a victim

Repentance without change is not repentance.

- True repentance is a turning away from destructive behaviors and then turning towards something valuable.
- Think of the last thing you said, "I am sorry" about and ask yourself, "Have I made provision in my life for a change?"

Sometimes we can't apologize

- If I repent to a bully for upsetting them, I can expect they will test me with another outrageous demand.
- I must say no and set up boundaries, otherwise, they will heat up the rage to prove that I am the unrepentant one.

Truth: Repentance should never give someone else the upper hand to manipulate you... again.

Remember: Love makes lasting changes...
Selfish people follow the direction of pleasing only themselves....

ENABLERS CAN REPENT FOR "ENABLING"

Here is what you could say:

It has come to my attention that I have hindered you from becoming a functional and responsible adult by doing too much for you. I would like to say I am sorry for this. I intend to empower you to become as independent as possible. Develop a plan for one week, two weeks, one month, or six months to disentangle financially.

- Let them know that you will never be responsible financially for the consequences to their irresponsible behaviors.
- Let them know you will not hire an attorney or bail them out of jail.

Leaving them in prison, could save their life. Confinement can allow them to sober up so they can intelligently make another choice for their lives. It may be the best thing you can do for them.

- Let them know any assistance plan you make with them is conditional. The plan will be abruptly abandoned if they are not working a recovery program.

Develop a backbone and demand progressive recovery!

Caution

- If they are resistant or argumentative, then say: "I have full confidence that you can do this." Give them phone numbers to rehabilitation facilities, halfway houses, shelters, food pantries and soup kitchens. Let them go. Some caught in hard core addiction cannot be helped but must find their own way.
- If you feel you are in danger and your boundaries will not be respected, you may need to get legal counsel or contact the police to determine what options you may have to extricate them from your home or to get back what belongs to you.
- You may need to acquaint yourself with shelters for abused individuals.
- You may need to hide money until you have enough to move away from them.
- You may need to borrow money to assist you in separating from an abusive situation. Seek legal counsel, if necessary.

ACCOUNTABILITY

1) Repeatedly, you can help your loved one out of the streets and into a rehabilitation center or a halfway house. It is his choice to take advantage of this and make better decisions. If he does not, is his brain scrambled with drugs? Is his thinking warped? Yes, definitely! The bigger problem could be your loved one is unwilling to place himself under the authority of others and accept instruction and work a program. Later, after the next high is gone and he is cold, wet and hungry, he may return for help to get into recovery. This can become a repeated pattern of failure. After two decades of multiple rehabilitation centers, and multiple attempts to intervene, the only choice may be to leave him in the streets. Email him the address and phone numbers of recovery centers. Work with the rehabilitation programs to let them know he may be coming. If he gets himself to a rehabilitation program and there is no enabler waiting in the wing, he may stay and work a recovery program.

Could they just as likely die in the streets? Absolutely! But, my attempts to assist one caught in hard-core addiction only interrupts whatever short recovery he was experiencing and precipitates the next relapse. So, I am not helping solve the problem by being sympathetic and financially assisting him. I am only prolonging his suffering. Financial assistance to get a person with SUD with one to two decades of drug abuse into a stable environment is difficult without assistance from court authorities. People who suffer from long term addictions need confinement to be safe from themselves. Working with their probation officer may be the best way to develop an accountability program. If they are driving and binging on alcohol or drugs, for the sake of every other person on the highway, arrange for their arrest. This is the responsible thing to do!

2) **Whatever the hardest thing for you to do, is probably the best.** In the 1990's, this was safer to do. But today's drugs are 1,000 times stronger. Our

laws need to be changed and significant others along with addiction doctors and counselors need to have the right to commit loved ones to a locked down facility when they are overdosing and near imminent death. Possibly if we could hold them accountable and get them sober, their heads would be clear enough to make the right choice and do the hard work of recovery. The younger we could implement tough consequences the more unpleasant they will find the addiction lifestyle.

Recovery is easier to accomplish before their thinking patterns are warped. Unfortunately, resources are severely limited, and the scope of the addiction problem is growing.

Regardless of how many attempts you make to get your loved one into rehab, never, never, never, give them cash. **Cash will usurp any willpower or decision-making power for them to make the right choice.** They will be driven to seek drugs again.

> Think of cash as the cattle prod to drive them to slaughter.

Now if you are an innocent, naive parent or grandparent and you keep making excuses for them and giving them cash to pay bills... well, they aren't paying the bills. They are buying drugs. If they are paying bills, it is with your money and that frees their money to be spent on drugs. *You, my friend, are the problem.* Your continual rescuing them from their irresponsibility will land you bankrupt and destitute and a great burden for others to care for your needs.

- Toughen up and disengage from the social problems other adults created by their poor choices.
- You cannot help those who do not want to do the work of recovery.
- **Your loved one's problem is not your problem!**
- Place the problem squarely on their shoulders and say, **"Well**

now, what are you going to do about that?"

3) When they come out of prison or rehabilitation facility, it is inadvisable for them to return to their enabler's home. Unless, they have established an accountability group and are willingly working with authorities (counselors, probation officers, sponsors, etc.) to do drug screens and to be held accountable. If they return to an enabler without accountability, it will interrupt your recovery as well as theirs. A better option would be a strong, supportive, structured half-way house with required meetings and counseling on a bus route. Then, they can find employment and pay their own bills.

CHAPTER 8: IS YOUR EMOTIONAL PAIN INSIDE OR OUTSIDE?

Being ruled by my emotions means my day will certainly be stressful.

Do you carry your pain inside, or have you learned to move your pain outside of yourself?

Symptoms of carrying pain inside

1. Fearful
2. Angry
3. Restless
4. Agitated
5. Impatient
6. Snippy
7. Negative and complaining
8. Feeling like a victim
9. Worrying
10. Anxious
11. Crying
12. Fretful

Severe Symptoms

1. Cutting

2. Medicating emotional pain with prescription medication or street drugs.

3. Overuse of alcohol or other mind-altering substances.

4. Mentally tormented and doing dysfunctional things to distract yourself from emotions.

5. Emotionally unavailable to loved ones.

6. Explosive and overreacting with exaggerated emotions. Passive/aggressive. Passive unless irritated.

7. Helpless syndrome. Victim mentality.

So how do I get this pain outside of me?

- If it is something I can fix or change, I do.
- If I do not know what to do, I go to an older trusted emotionally stable person in my life for counsel.
- If I still do not know what to do, I **wait** and do nothing until it becomes clear.
- I look outside of myself for help: counselor, AA, Al-Anon, Celebrate Recovery, Grief Recovery, or another support group.
- **If it is unchangeable, I accept it and STOP trying to fix it.**
- I **stop controlling** circumstances and outcomes in the lives of other adults.
- I empower myself by using healthy boundaries and saying "no".
- I learn to name my emotions, feel them, talk about them, and let them go.
- I learn that some things are broken, and it is ok.
- I recognize obsessing/negative thinking and focus on the positive things in my life.

- I start investing in safe people in my life who do love me and want to be close to me especially children.
- **I learn to be a safe person** for others to love by going back and mending fences and saying, "I am sorry".
- I make restitution where necessary. I pay back what I have borrowed or stolen.
- I make well thought out plans. I am not impulsive.
- I learn skills to resolve conflict. **Conflict cannot be resolved with one in active addiction or intense stubbornness.**
- I learn not to be afraid of conflict but to guard my heart from contentious people and to distance myself.
- I meditate on good words, good thoughts, and take those negative racing thoughts and place them in the garbage and refuse to think them.
- I tie my money up where I cannot get to it easily.
- Except for a couple dollars, I do not carry cash.

Stopping my fretting

- Write down good thoughts on 3 x 5 cards and place them where they can be seen often.
- Sometimes I write down negative thoughts and analyze whether they are true.
- Stop fretting.
- Refuse a negative thought and replace it with a grateful and kind thought.

This is not denial. This is an active listening to my thoughts, but not allowing them to control me. I observe my emotions as caution lights to slow down and process what is really going on so I can discern the root cause of the problem.

Tips for self-care

- I respect and accept myself and honor my weaknesses or injuries by taking care of me.
- I give myself permission to laugh and smile.
- I purpose to enjoy my day and use challenges to grow.
- I take every abusive thing that was ever said or done and forgive.
  - Forgiveness gives me the power to release the pain and move forward.
- If I am stuck, I refuse to isolate and turn inward and become overwhelmed.
  - Instead, I reach out to others even more.

Bad Habits

Sometimes my emotional responses are **bad habits**. I recognize them. I stop and mentally ponder what I have said. Then, **I make my own second chance**. I say, "that was rude, bossy, insensitive, etc." Next, I do the action or say the words the right way. This helps me overcome bad habits. It gives me time to think about it and learn internal controls to respond in a healthy manner. This makes a day so much more pleasant and alleviates stress and confusion in communication. This is also being a good example.

Ruling our own emotions, thoughts and attitudes is a **developmental skill** many of us have never understood or even knew was available to us. **Being ruled by my emotions means my day will certainly be stressful.**

Relieve your emotional pain

- Withdraw from those who are undisciplined.
- Mind our own business. Do not pry or meddle.
- Be quiet and busy taking care of your own responsibilities.
- Do not socialize closely with anyone who is irresponsible.

- Do not count this person as an enemy, but as one who needs firm correction.

GET THE FACTS QUESTIONNAIRE

Why do we need to distance ourselves from the unteachable? Answer these questions with a yes or no:

1) Does this person attempt to control my thoughts? (Usually he does this by repeating himself continually and getting louder and louder.)	
2) Does this person dominate or regulate my actions? (He tells me where I can go and who I can or cannot see.)	
3) Is there a repeated pattern of abuse?	
4) Does this person attempt to make themselves financially dependent on me or entangle me financially with joint bank accounts, co-signing, etc.?	
5) Does this person have constant excuses for why they can't work or can't keep a job?	
6) Does their money disappear everyday: fee, fine, robbery, suspicious expenses?	
7) Does this person lie to me?	
8) Are others (who love me) concerned about my over involvement with this person?	
9) Do they flatter and smile to get my devotion?	
10) Do they act helpless and come to me to rescue them?	
11) Do they dominate my life?	
12) Do they manipulate with emotions (crying, pleading, anger, or bullying)?	

Most importantly: Am I free to say "NO" to them without repercussions.

UNDERSTANDING THE ENABLER

CHAPTER 9: ENABLER'S CYCLE

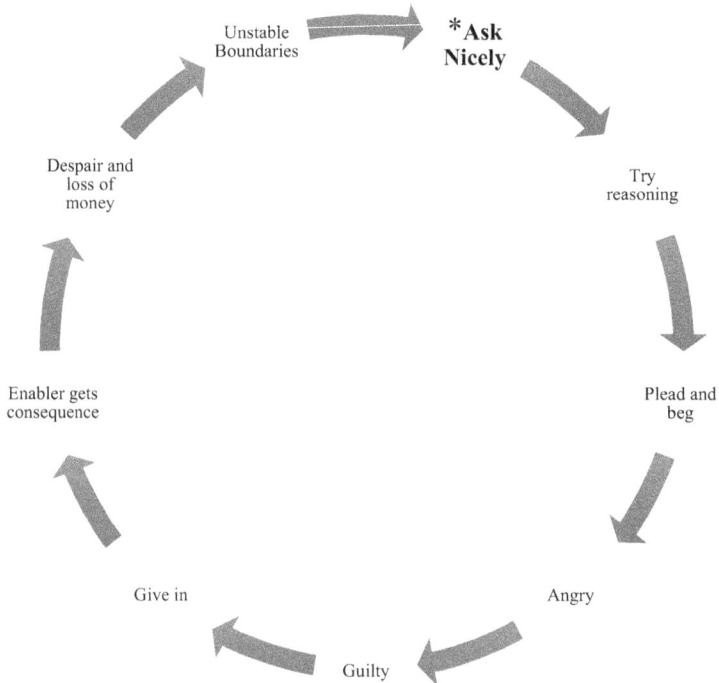

Unstable Boundaries

*Ask Nicely

Try reasoning

Plead and beg

Angry

Guilty

Give in

Enabler gets consequence

Despair and loss of money

Don't coddle irresponsibility and expect a responsible outcome.

Enablers are typically people pleasers. They want what is good and right for their loved ones. But they manipulate people and circumstances to extract good behavior. This type of a personality is overly responsible and fosters irresponsibility in others. First, look for yourself in these behaviors. Next, discern how these same behaviors are exaggerated and used against you.

ENABLER'S CYCLE AND TRUTH FOR RECOVERY

1. **Ask Nicely** - This could be normal behavior in a healthy family. However, the enabler is expected to do all the work in a co-dependent family. While the loved one with SUD only responds or complies to avoid a hassle, avoid conflict or play you for their next fix.

Truth

   - Individuals with SUD usually do household chores or yard work, so you are indebted to them. Not because they love you and want to be a functional member of the family.
   - Often, they promise to do work and ask for pay upfront.
   - Next, they stick their hand out with an entitlement attitude.

2. **Try Reasoning** - This is where you must coax an adult to stop drinking, work for their income, and to plan for their expenses. Your loved one will try this very reasoning on you. For example: If you don't bail me out of jail and get my car out of impound, I will lose my job and you will need to support me.

Truth

   - Who drove while intoxicated?

- Who got the car impounded because of a DUI?
- If you want them to learn the first time, it must hit them where it hurts with stern consequences.
- If the first timer must spend 6-12 months unraveling his consequences and paying his fine, he may not do it again.

3. **Plead and Beg** - This works both ways. If you pleaded and begged them to get out of bed this morning, they may plead and beg you for the car keys tonight.

Truth

- Respect their boundaries. If they say no, accept their no.
- BUT...there are consequences to actions. One consequence for not getting up is getting their bed taken away. They can sleep on the floor, on the porch, in the car, at the shelter, under a bridge or they can get up and go to work tomorrow.

4. **Angry** - Passive/aggressive anger is destructive to relationships. Trust me this behavior is learned quickly and comes back to haunt you. Deal with your anger. Make the rule patient, kind, but extremely firm with consequences for disobeying the house rules or rejecting your boundaries. Consistency is vital. If you are not in a place of power but are dominated by a person with SUD, it is necessary to plan to do the hard work to empower yourself to change your situation. Also, your controlled anger is appropriate until you can extricate yourself from the toxic relationship. Use silent and hidden anger to motivate you to change and develop stronger boundaries.

Truth

- Anger is to be used for protection and not to manipulate or coerce others emotionally.
- Anger can propel you to set up firm boundaries.
- Guard your tongue. **Angry words don't bring healing.**

5. **Guilt** - Work through your guilt and apologize   and make restitution, if necessary.

Truth

- Single parent, widowed parent, absent parent because of military, job duties, illness or divorce can cause a person to enable their loved ones to alleviate guilt.
- Watch for the **emotional guilt tactic** to coerce and embezzle financially from you.

6. **Give in** - Sometimes our boundaries are so pliable that our loved one with SUD will just keep pushing buttons until they can find the right one to make you give in and submit to their demands.

HOT BUTTONS

1. Whine, plead, cry, beg, pout
2. Angry, belligerent
3. Rationalizing
4. Blaming
5. Elevating selfish wants to need
6. Accusing you
7. Bringing up your past

8. Turning your words against you

9. Bargaining with you

10. Emotionally withdrawing or isolating from you

11. Relationship suicide (Cutting you off if they can't get what they want from you)

12. Self-destructive behaviors: cutting, reckless driving, etc.

13. Denial of the root problem: focusing on superficial, temporal issues

14. Making you the problem

15. Gossiping and slandering

Truth

- Detach emotionally from this person.
- Their brain is hijacked with drugs.
- They take hostages in relationships through **emotional entanglement.**
- **The quicker you can build walls around your heart...the sooner your decisions can be based upon what is best for you and them long-term and not what is easiest right now.**
- Tough consequences may cause them to wake up and stop their behaviors. But first, YOU MUST **GET OUT OF THE WAY and stop RESCUING!**

7. **Enabler Gets the Consequences -** The more you relent and rescue, the less likely they will learn. The more likely you will receive their consequences.

Truth

- Staying on the pathway with a person with SUD will bring certain financial and emotional ruin and maybe even physically devastate your health.
- It may also take them longer to recover.
- The longer they are on a path of irresponsibility the more ingrained the dysfunctional behaviors become and the more devastating the consequences.
- **Each rescue is only a temporary fix.** The next consequence will be greater and greater, until eventually the consequences will be so high, you will not be able to rescue them no matter how hard you try.

8. **Despair and Loss of Money** - When your finances are wasted, retirement savings gone and credit ruined, you will now be dependent upon others.

Truth

The path of addiction with another always leads to loss and destruction.

- Get your head out of the sand and disentangle yourself from this toxicity and salvage what you can before it is too late.
- Otherwise, you must find your own enabler to help rescue you from the consequences of impoverishment you received because of your enabling behaviors.
- You may even end up with a person who berates and belittles you day and night and have no viable means of leaving the situation.

9. **Unstable Boundaries -** Enablers are moveable. They are tossed about like

a little ship in a stormy sea. Their emotions are unstable. Their boundaries are unstable. Their decisions are unstable. Some enablers go without food or medicine. This is done so they can give their money away to an irresponsible person with SUD. Some enablers feel guilty if they don't give their money away.

Truth

Poor boundaries are like quicksand.

- If you lose your identity and you will be unable to control your addiction of enabling.
- Now find a stable, strong, dependable person to help guide you out of this mess!
- Trust this strong, dependable person to hold you accountable.

Sad Truth

This is not your beloved son, daughter, father, or brother. It is not them in front of you begging for money. It is alcohol. It is heroin. It is cocaine. Your loved one is hidden under addictive behaviors. Save your finances for a good, reputable rehabilitation program when they are ready to go. They will be ready sooner if they have no bed and are cold, wet, and hungry.

Rules

Never, never, never co-sign for them. Never place their expenses on your credit card. Never let them have your private financial information. Never borrow cash on your house to support them financially. Never bail them out of jail. Did I say...Never give them cash!!! If you feel you must pay child support, get a money order and address an envelope and mail it

yourself. **In case you didn't hear me…. Never ever give them cash! Most individuals with SUD cannot restrain themselves when they have cash in their hands. You may have signed their death warrant through overdose.**

> Every time you give a person with SUD cash you place another nail in their coffin.
> It is intense suffering to watch a loved one suffer.

WHY DO YOU ENABLE ADDICTIVE BEHAVIORS?

Things to think about:
- Are you enabling them to stop your suffering?
- Are you protecting your reputation?
- Are you in denial?
- Do you think you are helping?
- Do you think it is your responsibility?
- Do other relatives use guilt and shame tactics, if you do not enable irresponsible family members?

IRRESPONSIBLE ACTIONS OF AN ENABLER

- **Did you pay for an apartment, buy them a car and dress them up so they can pretend to be an honest citizen and find another unsuspecting victim to molest?**
- **This middle-class image will only lead to another beaten or abused lover, robbed employer, abortion, abandoned child, or even vehicular homicide.**

- **If you let a person who has had a previous DUI drive your car, you are responsible for the outcome.**

Truth

There is a steep price to pay to give your loved one privileges he has not earned and has previously abused.

MASTER ENABLER EXCUSE MAKER LIST

1. You need to not be so hard on him.
2. You cannot expect him to respect his teacher, boss, spouse, police officer, etc.
3. Everyone else has a car, he needs one too.
4. I will pay half; you pay half.
5. You know what will happen if you do not pay that fine for him.
6. The poor thing can come and live with me.
7. He can get more student loans so he can have his own place.
8. You should co-sign.
9. I paid for the car, now you pay the insurance.
10. He ran out of gas last night; you should get him a gas card.
11. He cannot work, he is sick.
12. That job is too hard for him.
13. Being a painter is beneath him.
14. He cannot do that job; he may hurt his knees.
15. Medicaid will take care of his needs.
16. He cannot work, he is mentally ill.
17. He needs Social Security disability.
18. The military would be too demanding.
19. It is just a phase; he will grow out of it.
20. Now, do not upset him, just go along with it.
21. You hurt his feelings.
22. If he stays on pain medications, he will receive more in his worker's compensation settlement and pain and suffering with his lawsuit.
23. You must pay child support, or he will go to jail.
24. You are a horrible person; you just want him homeless.
25. He cannot go to jail; he may get hurt.
26. He needs money in his pocket so he can feel good about himself.

27. He said he was sorry. So, do not mention it again.
28. I am going to the rehabilitation center and get him because he does not need to be there.
29. I am going to bring him to your house.
30. He needs new shoes, now what are WE going to doing about it.

What excuses do you hear yourself making for your loved one?

WHAT KIND OF AN EXAMPLE ARE YOU?

Half Truths	**Honorable**
Sometimes lie or speak half-truth to escape	Never lie
consequences for me or my loved one	Never cheat
Cheat on taxes or with insurance companies	Never steal
Do not correct an honest mistake if it is in my favor	Always honest
	Always kind and patient, but firm
Steal from credit card companies, employers Live above my means and have or need to file bankruptcy	Refuses to speak to liars and thieves until they repent
Motivated by Greed	Generous to responsible people and organizations
Motivated by selfishness (filing lawsuits for every fall or fender bender.)	Motivated by love (tough love, at times)

Motivated by what others think	Does what is right to protect a good reputation, but never compromises or goes along with what is wrong
Assist person with SUD to file false worker's compensation claims. Help manipulate doctors for their pain medication Give them your medication Drive them to the liquor store	Exhibits a strong work ethic Refuses to play manipulation games Refuses to allow anyone in the house who is under the influence of a substance Calls probation officers, police officers, and holds others accountable by arranging their arrest when they are out of control (This is love.)
Assisting person with SUD to file lawsuits for circumstances they complicated with their substance use disorder	Developing the courage to stand alone and do what is honorable, truthful, and right
Base decisions on what I think I can do without getting caught	Do right, even when no one is looking
Have I been a bad example?	Working a plan to continue my recovery and to be held accountable to others for my decisions

If our morality is full of half-truths, we can expect an exaggeration of our poor example mirrored back in our face.

ENABLER'S DYSFUNCTIONAL THINKING

1. I must keep the peace at all cost.
2. I focus on pleasing others.
3. I neglect my own needs.
4. My anxiety and stress are unmanageable.
5. I rescue others from their consequences.
6. I have lost sight of the ability to say "no".
7. I am fearful of the consequences my loved ones might receive.
8. I frequently micro-manage and control little things.
9. I flip between being passive and aggressive.
10. No one respects my boundaries, so I stop trying.
11. I feel helpless and sometimes hopeless.
12. I want good for my loved ones.
13. I manipulate others and frequently bargain or bribe them.
14. I am driven by guilt.
15. I am ashamed of my loved one's dysfunction and hide it from others.
16. I protect irresponsible loved ones by making excuses for them.
17. I am a "fixer" and a "people-pleaser".
18. I am frequently perplexed about what direction to go and easily controlled.
19. My life is full of confusion.
20. I do not have the energy to reach out and get help for myself.

Identify Skewed Thinking

This skewed thinking needs corrected! Turn around five of these statements. Example: I do not have to keep the peace.

TRUST SCALE GUIDE

Never give a person with SUD a temptation:
• Never leave your purse out.
• Hide your wallet.
• Hide your identity: Social Security card/Birth Certificate
• Count your checks and keep them under lock and key (a person with SUD may take a couple checks in the middle or end of the checkbook.)
• Never give passwords.
• Never give security codes.
• Never give house key.
• Never allow them to make a purchase with your debit/credit card.
• Never leave prescription medications unlocked.
• Never give them a key to the car. (Hide keys when not in use.)

| • Lock your bedroom door at night if they are in the house. |
| • Get an alarm system. |

Individuals in recovery need to earn trust: enablers and persons with SUD.

Are there other boundaries applicable to your situation? My boundaries need to be things within my control. For example: I will leave for an hour if you speak to me unkindly.

ENTANGLEMENT GAUGE	
Evaluate yourself and how entangled you are with an irresponsible adult:	
1. Providing Food	
Taking them out to eat frequently (or cooking for them)	
2. Providing Transportation	
3. Gas card	
4. Credit card	
5. Car insurance	
6. Health insurance	

7. Paying car payment or buying a car for a person with a history of DUI's	
8. Free (on demand) childcare	
9. Providing housing	
10. Paying rent or buying them a home	
11. Letting individual with substance use disorder live with you	
12. Picking up after them	
13. Doing their laundry	
14. Paying utilities	
15. Paying routine bills, cellphones, cable, internet, etc.	
16. Buying nice clothes	
17. Paying for haircuts	
18. Making excuses for them	
19. Co-signing for them	
20. Paying fees, fines, and other legal expenses	
21. Giving them false references for jobs	
22. Cashing checks for them or writing checks without reimbursement	
23. Paying unexpected bills: car repairs, doctor bills, prescriptions, etc.	
24. Paying for bad checks.	
25. Hiring attorneys to usurp consequences for irresponsible choices.	
26. Berating and bullying other family members to enlist help for the loved one with SUD.	

This scale will help you identify how deeply you are entangled with an irresponsible adult. Enablers with a "stand them up" and "fix them up" philosophy make their loved one with SUD appear to be responsible. This sets them up nicely to prey on unsuspecting victims. These victims could be left beaten, pregnant, abandoned and with their credit ruined within 4-6 months. It may also set up a person with active SUD to acquire jobs where they can abuse other employees and rob employers.

WHAT IS A HEALTHY RELATIONSHIP?

CHAPTER 10:TOXIC RELATIONSHIPS

People in toxic relationships give power away to gain power and control over another.

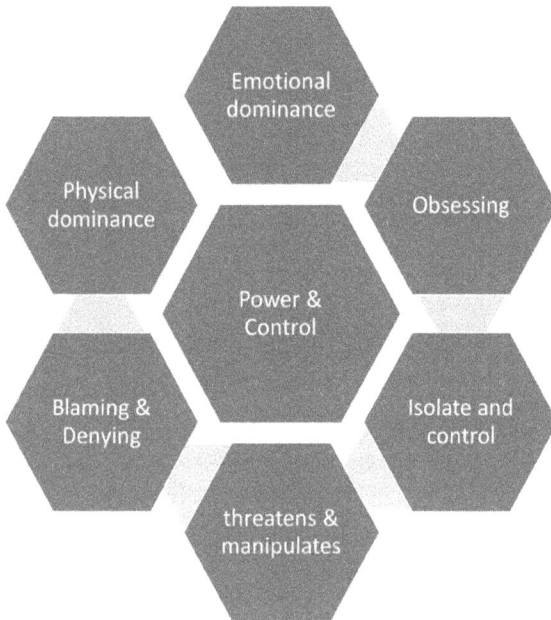

Eventually your power and control are completely taken from you.

You lose your own identity! If you keep hooking into the same type of dysfunctional people, you need to work on healing your emotional nervous system that subconsciously is attracted to toxic individuals. You may be attempting to repeat your traumatic past to resolve it or find a better outcome. This causes you to inadvertently repeat the same type of harmful relationships over and over.

TOXIC RELATIONSHIP WARNING SIGNS

1. Turns your words against you
2. Paranoid
3. Makes villains out of those who disagree with them
4. Uses intimidation
5. "If you love me" manipulation statements
6. Threatens to hurt you or others
7. Threatens to hurt themselves
8. Road rage
9. Escalates issues into a crisis when they do not get their way
10. Jealous
11. Excessive texting, calling, emails, visits, etc.
12. Insist you stop hanging out with other friends
13. Separates you from your family by being "offended" or causing an "offense"
14. Controls where you go, what you wear, and what you do
15. Complaining and discontent
16. Does not openly communicate problems
17. Refuses to resolve conflicts. Bears a grudge
18. Mood swings
19. Disrespects authority
20. Does not accept responsibility for their actions blames others
21. Frequently says:

- You should not say that
- You interrupted me
- You do not know what you are talking about
- You are stupid
- You are crazy

TOXIC RELATIONSHIP REVIEW

1. **Emotional dominance** - This abuser makes you second guess yourself. They twist words and pretend you are crazy. **They set you up to not even be able to trust yourself.** They play the victim to get sympathy. They tell you what you can think or not think, say or not say. You will frequently hear them say, "You shouldn't have said that!"

2. **Obsessing over having their own way** - Once the brain forms a negative loop of anxiety, fear, anger, or other intense emotion, it will obsess and repeat the torment over and over. You know your loved one is obsessing if they are verbally tormenting you with repetitive loops. They may obsess about money, employers, neighbors, or even trivial things like the way the dish cloth is hung or how straight the shoes are lined up. The longer they obsess the louder they vent. Their speech could be total lies, but eventually they will wear down their victim until the person gives in and agrees with them. **Disciplined thinking is greatly lacking.** This building of offenses is intentional to justify their next substance use binge or your next beating.

3. **Isolating and controlling you** - An abuser will slander and rail anyone in your life who could speak truth to you. They will separate and divide you from all healthy individuals. They use paranoia to control your thinking and alienate you from others. **If you are dating a person who dominates your thinking ...run!**

4. **Threatens and manipulates - A ranting, negative person uses anger to self-medicate. They use rage to release pent up emotions.** You may react and fight back, or you may retreat and become passive and make excuses for the abuser. Either one is unnecessary in a healthy, trusting relationship. If you

become your abuser's protector when natural consequences occur, (for example: domestic violence charges, assault & battery, arrest, etc.) you need more help than you can imagine. Go to a domestic violence shelter and ask about group counseling sessions. Go to counseling immediately.

5. **Blaming and Denying** – One in active addition does not take responsibility for their actions. They are contentious with anyone who attempts to hold them accountable. Individuals with SUD divide you and your other loved ones and play you against each other to have power to continue in their destructive behaviors without restraint.

6. **Physical dominance** - This physical dominance and control is never love. It is using and abusing. If you walk on eggshells trying to keep the peace, do not! Disentangle yourself from this relationship until they understand and seek recovery for their dysfunctional personality issues.

> Name calling the signature card of abuse.
> Blaming and playing the victim is the con game.
> An enabler is a master excuse maker.
> Stop making excuses for poor behavior and set up standards for your relationships.

HELPLESS SYNDROME AKA TOTAL TOXICITY

Feeling helpless can paralyze you from deciding and:
- Keep you overwhelmed.
- Bring on depression.
- Make you want to turn to an addiction.
- Give you insomnia, anxiety and/or severe physical illness because

of the chronic fight or flight syndrome which causes **enervation** (loss of strength or vigor).

<u>List for me what you will and will not tolerate in a relationship:</u>

Relationship Toxicity

There are times in the past few years I have felt forsaken, forgotten, lost and undone. I have felt I have heard the voice of reason only to have circumstances seemingly prove me wrong. The confusion and torment have been greater, longer, and harder to overcome than I ever imagined possible. The fear, anxiety and frustration has been intermittently incomprehensible.

Therefore, I find myself totally helpless. I always have choices, but sometimes no choice seems viable. So, my choice is to stay stuck in a cyclical pattern of abuse or choose to distance myself from the relationship and press onward and upward towards the peace I know can be mine. Sometimes, there are adults in our lives who take advantage and control us. They not only dominate our thinking but our entire life. We must emotionally set them aside and make the best decision for ourselves. This takes courage and emotional maturity. There is a skill we must develop where we toughen up and deafen our ears to their manipulative emotional ploys. Does this sound cruel? It is much crueler to continue rescuing than to allow them to face the consequences of their poor decisions. This consequence is theirs, and not ours. If we assume responsibility for the electric bill when they just spent $100 eating out last night, we are keeping them from experiencing the ramification of their choices.

| Who double-talks and usurps your decision-making skills?

Most enablers are greatly lacking in decision making skills. Other enablers know what decision needs to be made but lack the resolve to follow through with their choices.

Decide

- What sacrifices you are willing to make so your loved one can continue in addiction?

- What price are you willing to pay to keep them from suffering consequences?

- What cost is too high?
  Is it your health, safety, home, sanity, children, future security, stability, and/or your peace and quiet?

- What are you willing to sacrifice to make your loved one with SUD comfortable?

- What would your future look like if you changed?

- What will it look like if you do not change?

- What would it look like if you withdrew your emotional, physical, financial support?

- What are your greatest fears?

- What is the worse that could happen?

- What is the best that could happen?

CHAPTER 11: HEALTHY RELATIONSHIPS

Healthy relationships are intentional.

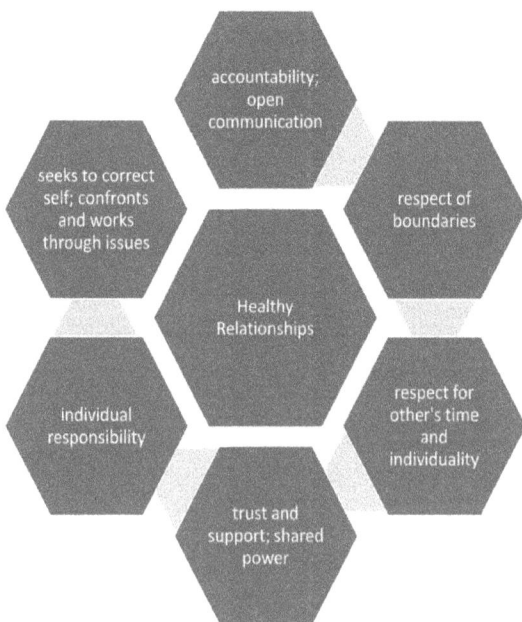

Is there such a thing as a healthy relationship? Yes, there is, but it takes work. Think of the goals you have for your relationships and plan accordingly.

HEALTHY RELATIONSHIP REVIEW

1) **Respect of boundaries - If I am not free to say "No", I will never be free to say "Yes"**. Practice respecting the boundaries of your loved one. A healthy relationship needs to ebb and flow and enjoy unity and togetherness as well as open healthy relationships with others. Secondary relationships need to compliment your primary relationships. There are several good books and resources on boundaries. If you have ever been abandoned, neglected, abused, or had your own addiction issues, much work will need to be done in this area. If there is confusion in the relationship, work to develop your own boundaries and respecting other's boundaries.

2) **Respect for other's time and individuality - No relationship is healthy without the ability to be an individual with our own personality.** I need to know where I start and where I end. If someone is always telling me what to think, eat, wear, say or do, I have lost my identity. Possessing my own identity is my individuality (likes and dislikes) and the ability to make my own decisions. **Healthy relationships are giving and taking.** They are a uniting of oneness and yet allowing everyone to have their own uniqueness. It is a respecting of another person's likes and dislikes. Both individuals in a healthy relationship will often yield their preferences to please the other. This yielding needs to be reciprocal.

3) **Trust, support, and shared power - There is no safe relationship without "trust".** If you cannot trust a companion, could you be with a foe and not a devoted friend? Support takes on different shapes: financial, physical, emotional, and spiritual. This too is reciprocal. If it is lop-sided, one may dominate in power and control and the other will feel frustrated and unloved.

4) **Individual responsibility - Serving one another without expectation brings great joy.** When both people within a relationship are evenly pulling the weight of the workload, the job becomes enjoyable. Think of yoked oxen. They must be evenly matched, or they will be chaffed, sore or even injured.

5) Seeks to correct self; confronts and works through issues - A teachable attitude intentionally seeks advise, instruction and counsel. When I can recognize and name my personal struggles, I can plan to change. When I am unable to change and keep falling back into dysfunctional patterns, I can be personally proactive and responsible to reach for outside counsel and accountability. Soon, I can discover the root issues and progress towards recovery. When the person I am with is safe to confront without taking an offense, things can be carefree, open, and growing. **Without the treasure of having a person in my life that genuinely cares about what I think, bitterness can fester like annoying splinters.**

6) Accountability; open communication - Secrets in healthy loving relationships are surprises for holidays or gifts. The relationship can never reach its full potential if you are hiding something, lying, or pretending. **The consequences of hiding and lying is a pervasive feeling of loneliness.** It is better to communicate regularly with your loved one. Let your partner hold you accountable in your weak areas. Ask for accountability (with a dash of grace, of course).

> If your partner uses your desire for accountability and open communication as a leverage to dominate you, find another trusted, safe person with whom you can develop accountability.

Also, some people lack insight into their own selves and can be emotionally illiterate. Communication gives them so much anxiety that they play avoidance games. This person can be emotionally unavailable and feel distant. Possibly they could be encouraged to work on their communication skills. Suggest counseling for them to begin identifying their emotions and develop their words to communicate in a healthy relationship. Don't force them to communicate. It will only push them away. It is not likely that they are even aware of their lack of connectedness.

STOPPING THE
CONFUSION

CHAPTER 12: DESTRUCTIVE DECISIONS

Protect your heart with all diligence from the confusion
and manipulation of others.

As our loved ones make destructive decisions, it is loving and natural to redirect them. But when the pattern of self-seeking, self-serving, manipulation for money becomes the norm, it is irresponsible for us to continue to make a loved one dependent upon us for deliverance from the consequences of their poor choices.

There are people with addiction behaviors you can guide to a recovery support group or a reputable rehabilitation facility.

SCENARIO #1: CAN I HELP THIS PERSON?

Here are some evaluators to help you decide:
1. They hate their substance use or addictive behaviors.
2. They are ready to do the work to get free, no matter what it takes.
3. They are setting up accountability for themselves and asking for more accountability.
4. They have every area of their life open for scrutiny.
5. They are going to recovery groups and have established a sponsor.
6. They are choosing different friends and rejecting people and places which are poor influences on them.
7. They are seeking employment or employed and developing a good work ethic.

8. They recognize their own weaknesses and are begging for rehabilitation and more accountability.
9. They are upset if they relapse and search diligently to find the reason for the relapse.
10. They are frequently in counseling.

This is one you can encourage and emotionally support (not financially).

◆ ◆ ◆

The **second person** with addiction behaviors we will discuss is a dangerous manipulator whose thinking and actions are dominated by some chemical addiction or immature impulsiveness and your very life may be in danger.

SCENARIO #2: CAN I HELP THIS PERSON?

Here are some evaluators to detect a person with addiction behaviors you cannot help:

1. They end up in crisis, no matter what you do.
2. They disregard their own health and safety.
3. They sell drugs to get drugs.
4. They steal from employers.
5. They steal from family and friends.
6. They write bad checks.
7. They steal your identity and open accounts.
8. They think their money is theirs and your money is theirs.
9. They induce crises by injuring themselves. They may burn, cut or stab themselves.
10. They manipulate doctors for prescription medication.
11. They tell incredible stories of being robbed, chased or beaten.

12. They leave or get kicked out of every rehabilitation facility or sober living house.
13. They have overdosed multiple times.
14. They have no remorse for lying and often play the victim to draw emotional sympathy.
15. They seem to have no conscience.

    If you are deeply entangled with a person with these types of behaviors and suspect you will receive the second scenario, it is best to seek your own counsel and to develop a plan for disentangling from them financially and physically. They will most likely end up in the grave or prison and you need to prepare yourself.

Prison could be a better option for them. It will give them time to evaluate their behaviors and a potential to reclaim their lives. **LEAVE THEM IN JAIL! DON'T BAIL THEM OUT!** It is the most loving thing you can do for them. The younger they are, and the sooner real-life consequences are faced, the more likelihood of recovery.

If they are on a drug or alcohol binge, you have an opportunity to work with probation officers and police officers to arrest and confine them for their own safety and the safety of the community. This is the responsible thing to do!

FREQUENTLY YOU CAN WORK WITH THE COURTS TO GET THEM TIME IN A REHABILITATION FACILITY in lieu of TIME IN PRISON. Use this opportunity to give them the chance to choose a rehabilitation facility. Ten days to sober up will be the minimal time needed. If they go to a rehabilitation facility in full blown withdraw, their anxiety will be too intense. They may not be manageable by the rehabilitation staff without a detoxification program.

- Some people are not safe to love.
- Love those with your head, do not give them your heart.
- Love them enough to do what is best for them and not what will appease

them temporarily.

- Love them from afar.

◇ ◇ ◇

When you withdraw yourself from being responsible for another adult's problems you can expect one of two scenarios:

Scenario One:

- calm resignation
- problem solving for other solutions
- increased responsibility
- making a financial responsibility plan
- seeking counseling or rehabilitation
- going to support group meeting

Scenario Two:

- exaggerated emotions
- bullying
- raging
- blaming
- arguing
- immediately seeking other enablers
- possible violence
- relationship suicide (where they cut you off)

DISTANCE YOURSELF EMOTIONALLY from unteachable ones who refuse to change.

Instructions

1. Distance yourself from those whose lives are disorderly.

2. Do not worry about another adult's self-imposed problems. It will only bring you suffering. **Mind your own business**.

3. Work on being "quiet" inside your heart and find work you enjoy.

4. Take notice of the person who is willful, wayward and unruly and distance yourself from them that they may correct themselves.

5. Do not count this person as an enemy, but as a loved one who needs to be corrected and held accountable.

6. Do not allow your thoughts to be consumed with the consequences of other's choices. Think about the situation for 5 minutes. If it isn't your problem and there is no power in your hands to stop or change the behaviors that keep causing the problems, push it out of your mind and enjoy your day! **Tip:** I literally set a timer for 5 minutes. After 5 minutes, I stop thinking about other people's problems, detach, and let it go. Letting other adults handle their own problems and/or consequences to their poor choices is emotional maturity for you and them.

DISTANCE EVALUATOR

Do we need relationship distance? Ask Yourself:

1. Does this person attempt to control my thoughts?	
2. Does this person dominate or regulate my actions?	
3. Is there a repeated pattern of abuse?	
4. Does this person attempt to make themselves financially dependent on me?	
5. Does this person have constant excuses for why they can't work or keep a job?	
6. Are they irresponsible? (poor work ethic, poor student,	

delinquent on child support, etc.)	
7. Do they overspend on eating out, cigarettes, and entertainment?	
8. Do they have poor money management skills?	
9. Does their money disappear everyday: fee, fine, robbery, suspicious expense?	
10. Does this person lie to me?	
11. Are others (who love me) concerned about my over involvement with this person?	
12. Do they flatter me and smile to get my devotion?	
13. Do they play the victim and act helpless and come to me for deliverance?	
14. **Most importantly: Am I free to say "NO" to them without repercussions.**	

Could it possibly be this person's manipulation is steeped in **mind control** over you? Have you lost not only your identity but are now being controlled by fear? Do you believe the false promises of a future of peace and love?

The purpose of distance is to bring peace and allow perspective. This lets you focus on others who want and need your help. You must also discern if this person will accept correction or if this abuser is entrenched in demanding his own way.

> When you are free from enabling, stand steadfast and do not be entangled again with them. Enabling makes you captive in the bondage of confusion.

My motto here is **"Don't feed the bears."** When a bear approaches a car and acts sweet to get food, he will become aggressive when your food runs out and you have to say "no". A person with severe addiction behaviors can be the same way. They may appear sweet, innocent and hungry. But if you consistently give to one in active addiction, they will come to expect it. Expect to be bullied when you have to say "no" to preserve yourself.

BONES

Does your loved one throw you a bone? Watch for these subtle techniques of manipulation which keep you coming back. The bone is a pretense action or statement to give you the love, respect, and comfort you deserve. **Watch out!** Once you take the bait, you will be entangled again in their game and the manipulative rebel reappears. It is important to see their actions and discern their motives and not to listen to cheap words.

Subtle tricks of the chameleon

This person is an opportunist, he uses a different bone by being a different chameleon with every new opportunity. Chameleon can change colors to match his environment.

When he is with:

- A police officer, he identifies with them by becoming an informant.
- Grandparent, he acts like a helpless sixteen-year old victim.
- His Christian aunt, he quotes scripture and pretends to be converted.
- Drug dealers, he pretends to be a gang bully and a thug.
- A girlfriend, he vacillates between intense loving passion and physical and verbal dominance.

ENTITLEMENT ATTITUDE

1. Are their words confusing or tormenting and you no longer can discern the truth from a lie and now you believe their happiness is your responsibility?	
2. Are they a dreamer?	
3. Do they have lottery mentality and think they will get a big settlement from a worker's compensation claim, insurance claim or disability?	
4. Do they want financial gain without working for it?	
5. Do they continue to chase a dream of fame and riches without any plan to provide for themselves and their family?	
6. Do they have a hundred excuses as to why they cannot work or keep a job?	
7. Do you feel like a powerless puppet? Do you do the same things repeatedly and think the result, this time, will be different?	
8. Do you think legal accountability and "just" consequences are bad and should be avoided?	
9. Do you lay awake at night worrying about someone else's problems?	

Is there someone who dominates your thinking and robs you of your peace? Reject them.

Otherwise, be certain your loved one with moderate to severe addiction behaviors will come every few days with another immediate financial need to obtain your paycheck, social security check, retirement check, etc. They arrive promptly on payday to deceptively embezzle your money for their dysfunctional coping needs.

CHAPTER 13:
MANIPULATION

Reject manipulation and stubbornness!

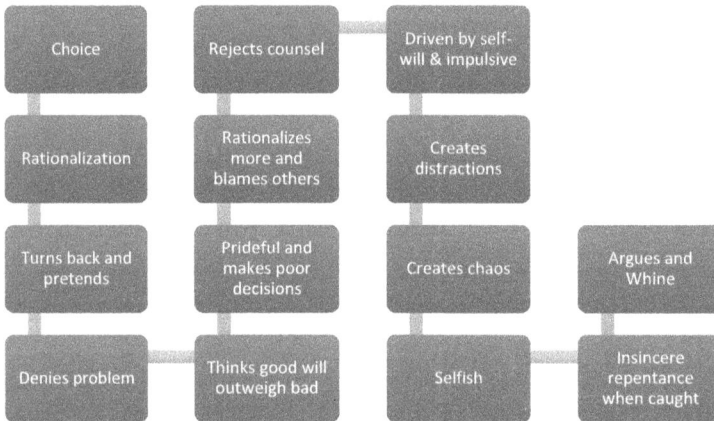

Choice	Rejects counsel	Driven by self-will & impulsive	
Rationalization	Rationalizes more and blames others	Creates distractions	
Turns back and pretends	Prideful and makes poor decisions	Creates chaos	Argues and Whine
Denies problem	Thinks good will outweigh bad	Selfish	Insincere repentance when caught

Let us analyze a conversation with a manipulator:

1) Manipulator: **Choice:** There will be a choice for the manipulator. They will blatantly disregard caution and make the wrong choice. "You wouldn't give me the money, so I had to take your credit card and use it."

   Me: **Consequence:** "You are going to pay back the money or I will file charges against you for theft."

2) Manipulator: **Rationalization:** The manipulator will make excuses as to why his way is best. "I needed the money and you wouldn't want me to pay a late payment."
Me: **Review Instructions**: "You could have paid it with last week's paycheck."

3) Manipulator: **Turns back and pretends**: When this doesn't work, he may dart his eyes around or furrow his brow. He pretends he didn't understand the instructions. "I thought you wouldn't care. I didn't want to wake you up."
Me: **Grieving:** "I am so sorry you are irresponsible."

4) Manipulator: **Denies problem:** He will deny wrongdoing. He will likely get louder and more aggressive. This tactic is used to back you down. "The bill wasn't due last week, and I had another problem come up.
Me: **Ask him to admit error:** "Did you budget your money and plan or squander your money on something else?"

5) Manipulator: **Thinks good will outweigh the bad:** A manipulator will think good will outweigh the bad. For example: Cheating is an acceptable behavior to achieve a good grade on the test.
Me: **Confronts with other problems:** "Why were you expelled from school?"

6) Manipulator: **Prideful and makes poor decisions.** I did not have time to go to class. My friends wanted to go out. I deserve to have my friends!
Me: **Instructs on planning:** Anything worth having is worth working

to obtain. If you start something, you should make a commitment to finish it.

7) Manipulator: **Rationalizes more and blames others:** He refuses to admit any error. "I didn't have time to study, and the guy next to me didn't cover his paper."
Me: **Confronts with other character issues:** "Have you paid your other bills this month? Do you think you should work more to pay the court fees paid on time?"

8) Manipulator: **Rejects counsel**: When a manipulator's problems are exposed, he will **blame** anyone or everyone for it. He will not take responsibility. "That woman I was with... she kept wanting to eat out."
Me: **Instruct on right choices:** "You could plan for things and live within your budget and make better decisions."

9) Manipulator: **Driven by self-will and impulse.** "I wanted to go out to eat, because everyone else was going to be there."
Me: **Suggestion solutions.** "You could have cooked at home for a fraction of the cost."

10) Manipulator: **Creates a distraction.** A manipulator can be expected to generalize and hide problems. "The judge hates me, and the courts keep adding fees."
Me: **Speaks what is right.** "The judge is holding you accountable for your actions and helping you mature and be responsible adult."

11) Manipulator: **Creates chaos.** "I can't find my shoes; you keep moving my shoes."

Me: **clarify words.** "I am not responsible for your shoes. I am not responsible for your bills."

12) Manipulator: **Selfish:** A rebel focuses on temporal rewards, not lasting value. "Who cares about stupid credit or an education anyway?"
Me: **Correct wrong thinking:** "I care about my credit and will not let you ruin it. An education is to be valued."

13) Manipulator: **Insincere repentance when caught:** A rebel when cornered will confess his mistake, but he is truly only sorry for the circumstances he is currently in and not for the behavior that got him there. "Ok, I am sorry! I will pay it back. Just don't file charges on me."
Me: **Achievable standard:** 'Ok, but it must be paid before my credit card bill is due, or I will file charges."

14) Manipulator: **Argues and whines:** "What kind of a mother are you? "You are the meanest person I know."
Me: **Stable boundaries with accountability**: "I am sorry you feel that way. If you are in a relationship with me, you will be held accountable for your actions."

This irresponsible adult needs to be distanced from you. These sort of double-talking, excuse-makers are going to have to learn on their own. This conversation is the norm with a person in active addiction. Sometimes individuals with SUD the conversation is about more severe consequences like abortion, divorce, bankruptcy, probation, and prison sentences. If you aren't getting anywhere and they aren't realistic, distance yourself and let them learn. Or your diamond ring will be at the pawn shop and your good credit ruined and your house will be sold to pay for money you borrowed to cover their irresponsibility.

> Don't pay bail! Whatever you do, don't co-sign for them!

Beware!

Anyone who is not accepting personal responsibility and becoming accountable and making amends needs to be avoided. The sooner you do this, the smaller your consequences will be. It is up to the person with substance use disorder to decide to become responsible or go find another enabler.

Beware! An active substance user is a compulsive liar. Don't believe anything they say without proof. We often say, "If he opens his mouth, assume he is lying." This helps us not to become wrapped up into ridiculous "victim" stories designed to reel us in. Instead, we detach emotionally and assume the stories are for manipulation purposes.

STEPS FOR HANDLING A MANIPULATOR

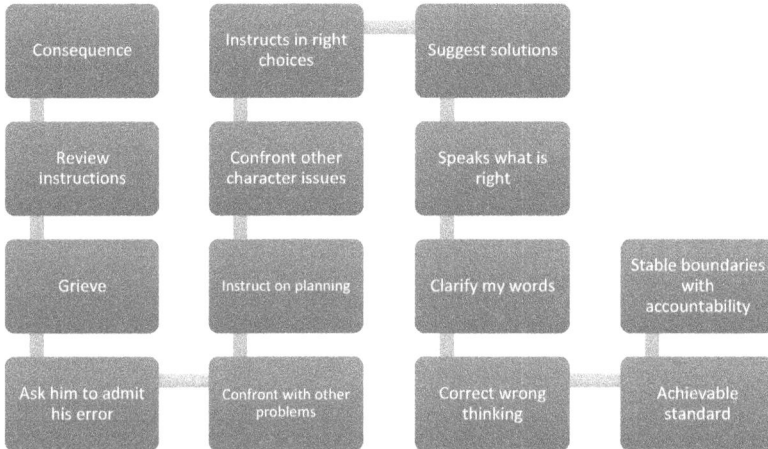

Consequence	Instructs in right choices	Suggest solutions	
Review instructions	Confront other character issues	Speaks what is right	
Grieve	Instruct on planning	Clarify my words	Stable boundaries with accountability
Ask him to admit his error	Confront with other problems	Correct wrong thinking	Achievable standard

These communication skills take practice.

If you can see their manipulation tactics, you will be less likely to be sucked into their emotional game. Then, you will have more energy for this healthy confrontation.

Confrontation (with kindness and patience) can be healthy!

THE GUILT TRAP: THE MASTER VICTIM ROLE

1)	Compares his life with others.
2)	Brings up your past.
3)	Turns your words against you.
4)	Manipulates what you say.

5)	Blames you or another for his problems.
6)	Gives a hard luck story.
7)	Self-pity: threatens to harm himself.
8)	Starving self or binge eating.
9)	Creates chaos for an excuse to use his substance of choice.

TEN THINGS TO CONSIDER BEFORE CONFRONTING A MANIPULATOR

1) **Make certain to deal with "all" your emotions before confronting another**. If not, you may become the abuser. If there are those in your life who are overtaken by addiction behaviors, be gentle and go to them with a couple of possible viable recovery plans.

    Motto: Patient, kind with firm, strong boundaries.

2) **Get control of exaggerated anger**. Anger only adds to their wounds and gives them an excuse to abuse themselves again.

3) **Irritations are a training ground for me to evaluate shortcomings and learn how to become a better person**. If I overreact, it is

    because I have not dealt with an old wound and my own emotions.

4) **Family members can be exaggerated mirror images of my own error.** Others around us tend to soak up our negative attitudes. If the problem is cyclical, search out any error or false belief and address the issues. *If I react with impatience, irritation, or any anger (even slightly) it is coming back at me… usually right away.*

    Motto: Low tone, slow speech but very, very firm "no" responses.

5) **Do not judge**. Do not judge or condemn them. This isn't love. Give them your full confidence that you believe they can overcome. Work on your own issues. Focus on becoming a better person. As you become healthier and have stronger boundaries, this may encourage them to change.

6) **Correct the stubborn**. The emotionally immature are stubborn. They are conceited and do not plan. Verbally play out the possible future consequences of their choices for them to hear.

7) **Do not correct the stubborn**. Some stubborn are so stubborn that any correction at all will give you an immediate and intense verbal or physical smack in the face. Ignore them and distance yourself.

These last two considerations require insight to know when to speak or not to speak.

8) **Correcting a hell-bent manipulator/rebel.** Any correction will be met with insults and incur abuse. This rebel will not accept instructions. He loves to argue. You could say the sky is blue and he would argue with you that it is green. **Don't waste your breath.**

9) **Do not reprimand the bitter or hateful.** No matter what you say, he will hear something different and hate you more for it. **Get out of the way the tornado is coming!**

10) **A sincere person can hear you!** *A sincere person will love you when you correct them and ask for more correction.*

Other things to consider

- Do I have a relationship with this person?
- Will they receive my correction?
- Are they under my authority?
- If not, are they asking for counsel?

It is very important to not correct someone who isn't under your direct responsibility. If I desire to help a person to learn, I can ask them this question: "If I see something in your life that might trip you up in the future, would you want me to tell you?" When I ask for permission, the person is engaged and ready to listen. I start with gentleness or a story about how I received a consequence and learned this lesson the hard way.

More things to consider

- If a person will not receive correction, they may come back later and ask for advice if you wait for an opportunity.
- Opportunities for teaching are good when the person is aggravated or frustrated and cannot figure out what to do in their life.
- Do not listen to gossip or slander and do not be a gossip or slanderer.
- If you are not part of the problem or the solution, do not listen to it.
- The only exception I make to this rule is: if I need to know what is going on to protect my family or myself.
- Do not stay in close fellowship with people who are unpredictable.
- Do not allow yourself to be dragged into the middle of someone else's problem.
- Do not get in the middle of an argument that is not yours.

- Do not be a busybody.
- If things are heated emotionally, walk away and come back later.

CHAPTER 14: EXPOSING A MANIPULATOR

Manipulators can confuse us and inhibit our maturity.

As we mature, we must address the manipulation that lives within our own hearts. This is done through continual self-examination or being involved in authentic relationships where we can sharpen each other and where the cautions and corrections of a friend are welcomed.

But it has come to my attention the manipulators in our lives (family, old friends, co-workers, mates, x-mates, or adult children) can derail our growth and keep us confused and inhibit our maturity.

1. **We need to be following truth.** I want you to have a solid and stable life of peace. I desire for nothing to inhibit your happiness. I am strongly jealous against the manipulator in your life who robs, derails, and distracts you from enjoying a pleasant day.

2. **Manipulators deceive and are crafty. They corrupt our minds from a simple life of love**. Each one of us have those who are trying to deceive us with which we must contend.

3. **There is a cheater who beguiles you with a myriad of enchantments.** Even if you accept this manipulator, your forbearance makes you vulnerable to constant chaos. The manipulator will trouble you with one tactic after another to entangle you again and again.

4. **Manipulators can transform themselves into respectable citizens** who pretend to have been victimized and need to be rescued.

5. **Manipulators play enablers and co-enablers against each other**. How can this be? They have perfected the art of manipulation.

6. **Cast the manipulator out of your heart**. This will allow you to see clearly with whom you are contending. Look at the facts only and this will cut off emotional manipulation. Actions need to speak louder than words. Love them with your head and not your heart. Some people are not safe to give them your heart.

More things to consider

- Do not add to your suffering by pretending nothing is wrong.
- Do not think you are wise and can solve their perpetual problems.
- Do not give them emotional control over you.
- Do not give into fear.
- Do not give them control or you will be the one in bondage.
- Do not allow a manipulator who steals in your home or your possessions will be at the pawn shop.
- If they have physically attacked you before, do not let down your guard.
- Do not feel sorry for them when they receive legal consequences for their actions.
- Do not steal for them.
- Do not place yourself under the authority or in the home of a manipulator. If you are living with a manipulator, secretly start saving income and making plans to be independent.
- If you are being physically abused, find a safe place or a domestic violence shelter and retreat.
- Do not ever leave children with immature, manipulative or selfish

caregivers. That is a recipe for disaster.

Questions to ask yourself

Is there a manipulator in your life who causes suffering and you are tolerating them?

Is this person bringing you into bondage? (Mentally, emotionally, physically, spiritually, or financially)

Do they make you feel confused and incapable of saying "no", even when you have purposed to do so?

Do they boast about themselves or put others down?

Have they ever hit you?

Manipulators can be first class professional cons and sophisticated embezzlers.

Manipulators can prey on good people and pretend to be guiltless victims of circumstance. I say... open your eyes and recognize them. Let truth strip them of their masks. You do not have to bear with them. Let no person spoil your enjoyment of a simple life. May your eyes be open to see the ideology they are teaching. May you refuse to suffer menacing manipulators in your life. May you escape the bondage you are in. This bondage may be physical, but it started mentally and emotionally, and you will not be free until you truly see the identity of your abuser. They are deceptive serpents and selfish manipulators. The one you loved is not there. Only when you stop coddling the idea of who you think they could be and see them for who they really are can you be free. Now, if you refuse to believe all the lies and excuses, maybe they can mature and recover themselves.

> People with moderate to severe addictive behavior lie constantly. Do not believe anything they say without proof.

Trapped in a toxic relationship

Plan an escape:

Mentally: When thinking is dominated, you spend mental energy imagining a way to convince others why their actions model insanity. Then, obsessing over what they should or could have done is common. When this happens, you have lost your freedom to enjoy your day.

Physically: When you run to get a manipulator out of their distress, it isn't helpful. You have rescued them many times, and it doesn't help. If they are worse and it has been ten years, for the sake of your sanity --- leave them. Remember the **"law of reaping and sowing"**. In my experience, rescuing from consequences produces more devastating consequence because they didn't learn from their mistakes. Eventually, the consequences will be so drastic, you will not be able to rescue them from the repercussions of careless living.

Financially: If you are entangled financially, make an immediate plan to disentangle yourself from being financially responsible for irresponsible adults. This plan could be as short as one month or a year or more. Move irresponsible adult children out of your basement!

> Do not coddle adult children and allow them to wander on the path to nowhere!

If they have money to spend on enabling others, drugs, alcohol, gambling or pornography, they have money to live independently. If they choose to spend their money frivolously, it is not your problem. Let them learn early to be financially responsible.

If they live with you, they must pay rent, utilities and buy their own food, do their own laundry and clean up after themselves. If you like, you can save this money for them to give to them for a down payment on their own place or on a car. This is something you should not commit to and only do if they have earned it with responsible choices for a significant amount of time. Don't do anything for adults with addictive behaviors that they should do for themselves (laundry, clean their car, iron their clothes, make their bed, etc.). Don't do anything for them that they squander (paying for college with failing grades).

> Don't do anything for them that responsible adults could/should do for themselves. This will rob them of their dignity and independence.

If you have a person in your past or present who fits this description, you may be mentally and emotionally in bondage or have post-traumatic stress even though you are free from them physically. My dear friend you need courage and strength. May you have boldness to completely disentangle yourself emotionally, physically, and financially and receive complete freedom from this intense suffering. May you spend your resources getting yourself counseling and care, so **you** may recover.

> ACCEPTANCE of their right to make their own decisions and allowing them to suffer the consequences of their own poor choices will give you your life back.

Oh, and by the way, it will get worse before it gets better. The intensity of all the games of manipulation and the incredible stories of their victimization will escalate. Be prepared!

And then REMEMBER to POST THESE WORDS NEAR YOU!

> A "leg-up" for responsible young adults, or the working poor is one thing, enabling a perpetual pattern of addiction or irresponsibility is another.

Conclusion

Manipulation is rebellion. It is the pathway to destruction. Should we stay on a path with our loved ones in rebellion? No, not unless we want their destructive consequences.

Is there another person in your life that is precious and innocent and does want your support and counsel? Is there one who will make responsible decisions and not take advantage of you? It would be wiser to invest in this person. Sometimes the enabler will get so consumed trying to save one family member from their destructive decisions that they lose sight of the other family members who simply want to love them.

Things to ponder

- Don't let manipulators have easy access to you.
- Intentionally separate yourselves from them.
- Don't rationalize what is wrong could be right.
- Don't make excuses for them.
- Step back from the relationship, until you see a changed life over a

significant amount of time.

> Protect your heart from all stupidity. Make decisions with your intellect and not emotions.

Should I continue year after year in close relationships with manipulative people?

If you have worked with them and counseled them, loved them and served them for ten years and they are worse. For your sanity's sake, and for the sake of all of those around you that do love you and will hear you... I give you permission to **DISTANCE** yourself from the rebels in your life.

The **purpose of distance** is not only to bring us some peace and give us perspective but to let us focus on others who want and need our love and assistance. A second purpose for distance is so the person will feel remorseful and seek to change.

So, ask yourself, why do we pacify manipulative people?

Do we allow a manipulative person to control our thoughts or our actions?

Do we give our power to undeserving people who rob us of our peace?

Do we make excuses for manipulators or those in rebellion?

Past Abuse

- Could it be this manipulative person has stolen my "identity"? Even now my mind is being controlled by bullying, fear, threats, or even flattery. I must align my thinking with rational truth. As a victim, or a co-dependent enabler, it is easy to forget that I have the power to walk away.

Being a martyr may be noble to save the life of another. But the truth is I am sinking in their quicksand of stupid choices.

Could a manipulator in my past still control my present and future? If so, am I stuck in an **emotionally immature dependency cycle** waiting for the approval of another. Counseling is needed or I am likely to repeat the cycle with a different name, face, and place.

- Are you, also, consumed with guilt, bitterness, anger or resentments? If so, we need to forgive and let go of the past and move forward. *This is our best chance for healing.*
- Does the fear of future consequences for our loved ones plague us? The sooner we let them go, the smaller the consequences will be for us. This is an act of trust. Get counsel. Get support. The sooner we let go, the sooner we can recover. The sooner they may want to recover.

Fear of the future robs you of today.

- Has holding onto bitter past abuse robbed you of today?

- Does a past circumstance identify and drive you to make unhealthy decisions?

Current Abuse

- Have we heard the words of torment so long that we can't discern truth from a lie?
- Does the abusive person "throw us a bone"? Is he sweet and kind to manipulate us? Don't mess with people who are temperamental. Once you become entangled (emotionally, physically, financially) the game is on and the rebellious manipulator reappears.

May you find emotional, physical, spiritual, and financial freedom from your own compulsion to rescue others. May you be free from all the suffering of manipulation. May you always be free to say "no" and walk away.

CHAPTER 15:
UNDISCIPLINED THINKING

Undisciplined thinking is our greatest problem.

My Previous Undisciplined thinking: (it was accompanied by compulsive manipulation of people and circumstances)

1. Despair of the future
2. Suicidal thoughts
3. Depression
4. Discontent
5. Anxiety & constant worry
6. Fear (with torment)
7. Doublemindedness
8. Overwhelmed
9. Racing negative thinking
10. Pouty/Broody
11. Melancholy
12. Daydreaming escape thinking
13. Contentious
14. Confused
15. Stubborn & rebellious
16. Hopeless
17. Untrustworthy (I certainly couldn't trust myself.)

As I searched for reasons for my mental instability, I realized my thinking was irrational and uncontrolled. **Undisciplined thinking was my greatest problem.** I indulged every sick and sorry thought or emotion that came my way! I either lived repeating past trauma or imagining future tragedy. When I recognized this pattern, it became a crossroad for me.

- Am I going to live my life in fear and anxiety?
- Am I going to take charge and stay in the present moment and enjoy my day?

Currently, I am at the beach listening to the rhythm of rolling waves. In the past, I would not have allowed myself to enjoy such a beautiful day. But today, I have only hope and dreams of goodness, kindness, and recovery for the many of you reading this book. I am focused on your healing and sending you my love. You too, can find deliverance from all your undisciplined thinking.

First, you must be intentional about what you do and do not allow yourself to think.

- Are my thoughts about past things I cannot control?
- Are my thoughts focused on future unpredictability?
- Am I trying to think hard enough about a circumstance to attempt to change something that is not my responsibility to change?
- If I am worrying non-stop about how to get my loved one sober and/or responsible, my suffering is extremely intense, and my thinking is futile.

What to do

1. I want you to get alone and set a timer for five minutes and grieve as hard as you need to grieve. This can be a literal "death wail". Detachment and letting go of our control is hard work.
2. Then I want you to get up and refuse any thought about the

circumstance or situation you cannot change and enjoy your day.

3. If your thoughts are obsessive and you cannot stop them, tie a positive thought around your neck with a string and 3x5 card and say it to yourself every time you catch yourself thinking negatively.

4. Sometimes it takes a hundred times of saying a good thought. "I have hope. I have courage. I have strength," before I can break a negative thought pattern.

5. But with practice, I can be singing and enjoying my day.

6. If I get overwhelmed again, I mourn and grieve for 5 minutes and then detach from what I cannot change and purpose to enjoy my day.

7. When I did this, I found sweet little children at my feet who needed a smile and a hug. I heard the birds sing and was able to enjoy flowers again.

8. I give you permission to be a little selfish and take time to care emotionally and physically for yourself.

9. The undisciplined thinking makes me grumpy. This all disappears when I take charge of what I allow myself to think and feel.

10. I can't do this unless I am calm and give myself enough space to think, feel and process my emotions and let them go.

Suddenly, this enabler with undisciplined, impulsive, negative thinking has become an anchor of stability for others to cling to in their storm.

IDENTIFYING TRUE LOVE

CHAPTER 16: HIGHER AND LOWER LEVELS OF LOVE

Beloved means: one who is greatly loved.

DEVELOPMENTAL STAGES OF LOVE

Lower levels of love

1. **Self-love** – empty, lonely, using others. Characterized by a life of confusion.

2. **False Love** – kind speech in mouth, but not in heart. This type of love is very irritating.

3. **Enabling Love** – This person understands consequences and tries to remove the mountains in other people's lives. Most usually these mountains are very important so that the person can grow and mature and become strong. This person has faith, but their faith is usually in themselves or in their money.

4. **Best Effort Love** – This person does a lot of charity work and gives of themselves. They do this to look good or to make up for other

things in their lives that are not right. This type of love can be motivated by guilt or a need for approval and acceptance.

Higher levels of love

Understanding my purpose in life

5. **True Love** – Patient and Kind. This person wrestles their own stubborn self-will and pins it to the ground and pursues being a person that loves this way. **This person repents often.**

6. **Tough love** – This love is strong enough to allow others to have their own free will and make their own choices and suffer their own consequences. This person trust that others can find their own path.

7. **Perfect Love** – Characterized by having no fear. Speaks truth to himself frequently and wrestles fears and pins them to the ground.

8. **Love your Higher Power and your neighbor as yourself**. This love is pure and seeks opportunity to help those in genuine need.

9. **Love with great peace** – This person will never take an offense. But he will instead, bear the burden of others. This person visits the sick and makes meals for those with cancer or with a new baby. This person keeps their schedule loose enough to plan for the little interruptions in life.

10. **Everlasting love** – This love transcends time, space and all eternity and will love forever. This is a love that is more powerful than life. This is a place of safety and honor. When there is higher level of

faithful, devoted, selfless reciprocal love and devotion, you can find someone you can greatly love and be someone's beloved.

Finding mature love means letting go of the lower levels of love. This will allow you the capacity to give and receive higher levels of love.

THINK EFFECTIVE BOUNDARIES

- **At times, you may need to draw near your loved ones.**
- **At other times, you may need to move back from them to allow them space to work through the developmental stages of love.**

Here are some behaviors to identify true love from false love:

Love is….	Love is never….
Peaceful	Demeaning
Gentle	Demanding
Kind	Abusive
Rewarding	Neglectful
Caring	Manipulative
Sharing	Hateful
Patient	Argumentative
Forgiving	Vengeful
Always wanting best for others	Controlling; demanding own way
Working it out together	Fearful
Talking it out together	Full of should & shouldn't

Respectful	Resentful/Bitter
Trusting	Accusatory
Forgetting the past	Never forgetting the past/shaming
Giving and Helping	Selfish/self-centered
Always thinking of how to encourage others	Discouraging
Always uplifts another	Tearing down the esteem of another
Allows freedom to make their own choices	Yelling and angry
Allows person to receive consequences for poor choices.	Manipulates other people emotionally and bullies to get them to do what they want
Hopes for the best	Denies there is a problem
Refuses emotional manipulation	Accepts consequences or interrupts them (enabler)
Gets wise counsel, ponders each word spoken and each deed done.	Decisions based on emotions
Seeks help for self when stuck emotionally	Throws money at a problem to "fix it"
Sets standard and a plan	Makes excuses for themselves and others
Sticks to the plan Accountable	Smooths things over
Willing to suffer for right decisions	Hides things
Willing to avoid rebels if	Everyone must get along at

needed	all cost
Always kind, but firm	Easily manipulated
Backs up words with actions	Angry
Always does the next right thing	Anxious
Is not manipulative and does not manipulate	Confused
Holds others accountable	Poor boundaries
Committed to doing what is right	Chaos
Respects individuality	Dominate and controlling
Harmonious	Passive and Double-minded
Teachable	Not interested in learning
Gentle	Prideful

> If you expect mature devoted love, you must be a whole enough person to receive it.

When you are working with immature people with lower levels of love, use your boundaries to choose loving responses. Do not mirror their behaviors, instead use your cognitive reasoning to resolve to love them by allowing them to experience their own suffering. Suffering, if we accept it, can work us through these stages at a faster pace.

FINDING EMOTIONAL
MATURITY

CHAPTER 17: EMOTIONAL IMMATURITY VS. FULL EMOTIONAL MATURITY

People experiencing any type of addiction experience emotionally exaggerated feelings and destructive behaviors.

What are the signs and symptoms of a life of immaturity?

A child does not have the moral capacity to understand his emotions and parent himself through the truth. An adult walking in **exaggerated emotions of immaturity** has missed this stage. The goal is to retrain our thinking patterns and break the many lies that bind us in destructive behaviors and become emotionally stable and mature. People experiencing any type of addictive behaviors usually experience emotionally exaggerated feelings and destructive behaviors. Enablers exhibit some of these behaviors at different levels. Mark any dysfunctional emotions or behaviors you need to examine and work through to resolve.

<u>**Exaggerated immature emotions**</u>

- Bitterness
- Vengeful
- Conditional love
- Fear/Paranoia
- Conforming because of fear (not love)
- Decisions based upon fear of what others think
- People pleaser
- Tears down relationships (negative, nagging, abusive words)

- Bullies
- Cuts off people who can't be manipulated
- Learns survival skills of aggression
- Curses authority
- Turned over to dangerous thinking and actions
- Discontent
- Slanders/Gossips
- Takes hostages in relationships (controls and manipulates)
- Holds grudges
- Takes advice from no one
- Runs/Hides/Diverts blame
- Tormenting thoughts
- Scattered/unfocused thoughts
- Grandiose thinking
- Undisciplined sensual thinking
- No long term goals
- Easily discouraged/fainthearted
- Waste time
- Stability and/or sobriety seems allusive
- Lazy
- Never satisfied
- Double-minded thinking/unstable
- Double talking
- Stumbling without direction in life
- Easily led astray
- Indulges in berating self-destructive negative thinking
- Embraces and mulls over negative emotions
- Wallows in self-pity
- Poor decision-making skills

A life full maturity?

If I clean up my compulsive thinking and my impulsive responses and replace them with right thinking and right responses, I can find emotional stability and security.

EMOTIONAL STABILITY

- Unconditional love
- Healthy strong boundaries
- Healthy identity
- Actions show responsible and mature love
- Joy/Contentment
- Builds healthy relationships
- Serves others: patiently caring for children, handicapped, and elderly
- Learns to distance yourself from negative people, places and things.
- Supports those in authority and encourages them
- Protected from manipulators by very strong boundaries
- Holds no grudges
- Chooses to build trust and respect
- Repents frequently & forgives easily
- Makes the best of suffering
- Uses bad circumstances as growing experiences
- Honors (only the honorable) in parents, employers, co-workers, etc.
- Confronts and deals with issues
- Waits patiently for good to come
- Mind is disciplined and peaceful
- Senses imbalance and corrects self quickly

- Focused
- Purposeful goals and plans
- Persistent/Diligent
- Uses time productively
- Plans for future stability
- Yields to authority (becomes excellent follower or leader)
- Perseveres
- Seeks counsel for needed change
- Does not give in to emotions
- Deals with emotions constructively
- Seeing things with your eyes open (not excusing liars, thieves, etc.)
- Walks in the love, joy, peace, and self-control
- Chooses right no matter what the cost.
- Refuses grumbling and complaining
- Purposefully practices gratefulness daily
- Embraces quietness and stillness
- Faces challenges with courage... no matter what!

I have some work to do.

Name five things you would like to work on in your life:

What are some practical ways to do this?

EMOTIONAL MATURITY

If we want emotional maturity, we must develop our self-control.

> Self-control over our speech and thoughts can establish us as an impenetrable fortress.

I will not say it! I will not even think it!

This requires a purposeful planning and studying of my thought patterns and healing my brokenness and traumatic memories. Otherwise, I am overreacting to everyone and everything. If I am spending time in quiet reflection and meditation daily, I will have a mental shelter to withstand any storm.

> Meditation is like a mental shelter to withstand any storm.

When I am weak

- My emotions are in control. I know this is happening because I can hear myself whining, nagging, complaining, and discontent which fuels my negative emotions.
- When I recognize I am stuck in this trap, I shake myself and remember my goals. I want a pleasant, enjoyable, happy day.
- This means I must choose every thought, word, and action and shape them with positivity and sound reality.
- If I can't get free from mental torment, I am stuck! I call a professional counselor and make an appointment or go to a support group meeting or both.

> Developing patience and self-control in no way makes me a doormat.

These character traits empower me:

- to choose to distance myself from toxic relationships.
- to see negativity and chaos coming and hide myself from it.

- to keep my mouth shut with people who cannot hear correction.
- to have reflective thought and gentleness when confronting someone.

Now, I can make room in my life for safe people.

> This type of emotional maturity gives me the strength and courage to go to higher ground.

For example: If my boss is blaming me for something he did and trying to make me look bad, I can respond with his ugliness or I can claim whatever % is my responsibility. Then I can apologize for it and ask him for suggestions to amend the error. This gentle attitude usually throws him off guard. The kinder and more patient I am with him, the more he may recognize his imbalance and the more likely he is to return to me and apologize.

When a person follows your example and returns to apologize, here are some things to think through:

- It is important I have not held onto any grudge or bitterness against them.
- But instead, consider the pressure they are under and the struggles they are facing that would make them attack a person in such a way.

You see, most often **it is not about me**. It is about the frustrations in their life that they have not dealt with properly and it's boiling over on me. My soft answer, if they repent, is to say, "I didn't take it personally, I can't imagine the pressure you are under. I am here to do anything I can to make your day easier and support you." Talk about employee of the month! The only way I can do this is if I have emotional balance and stability and am not easily teetering off someone else's negativity.

If they do not say they are sorry, act as if nothing happened and go back the next day with a fresh smile and a supportive, encouraging word. Your attitude may earn their trust. If nothing else, you still have your sanity and haven't lost your peace over someone else's emotional imbalance. This type of response will help you **build empathy for others**. Balance this with not enabling them to abuse you or others, but with an emotionally mature response where you go to "higher ground" above your emotions and theirs.

The mountain goats graze effortlessly on the side of the mountains. Their feet enable them to overcome the slopes and give them stability on "higher ground" to graze on the luscious green grass. They never stagger or stumble. There feet are nimble, and their positions are fixed. Now use this image to train yourself to go to "higher ground" emotionally.

| Go to higher ground emotionally.

This maturity skill requires you to respond in an opposite attitude than you would naturally respond. It requires cognitive thinking and purposeful choosing to not be sucked into trauma-drama games, but to live your life on higher ground in an emotionally stable manner.

Do you see the imbalance in the boss and how you could keep your balance and stability despite anyone else's imbalance? I call this "owning" my own identity.

Now, take this example and work out a scenario for other relationships with imbalances:

Few bosses have employees who support them during their stress, no matter what! Your other option is to become part of the problem and grumble or gossip. Trust me, this will not end well.

> Grumbling breeds an environment of discontent that is stressful to endure and drains all your energy.

Refuse boss bashing. Refuse to participate in speaking or listening to gossip or slander from co-workers. Refuse to listen to negativity about anyone in your family or even about the person with severe addictive behaviors. If you aren't part of the problem or part of the solution, don't allow others to engage you in negativity. Think the best. Hope for the best. **Now, be emotionally mature enough to stay out of the way.** If others draw you into a three-way offense, they will suck you back in emotionally and end up blaming you for their next problem. Just steer clear.

If an individual with SUD is attempting to engage you in a conflict, ask yourself: Whose problem is this? Then do not usurp their growth experience. Instead, ask: "Are you asking for my advice?" Make sure you are giving them back their problem and you **show no emotions**.

QUESTIONS TO FACILITATE GROWTH

- What did you do to get yourself in this position?
- What can you learn from this experience?
- What will you do differently in the future?
- Is this something that has tripped you up before?
- Who are you going to be accountable to for this?
- Do you need stronger boundaries on yourself?

- How could you make restitution?

One of the greatest compliments I ever received from one with SUD was "you are always the same." **Negative emotional games have temporary pretend power, but end in confusion and brokenness. Patient, firm, kind, loving responses give me stability and self-control.**

As I practice emotional stability of patience and kindness, I can enjoy my life.

IDENTIFYING IRRATIONAL COPING

Do I have discernment, or do I have irrational coping skills?

- Isolation
- Fear
- Anxiety
- Anti-social behaviors
- Presumptuous
- Withdrawn
- Stuck
- Lonely
- Avoidance
- Offended

DISCERNMENT

- Reject every negative thing
- Hopeful

- Releasing control over others
- Controlling my thoughts and speech more
- Healthy boundaries
- Patient and kind
- Not taking responsibility for another adult's problems
- Not manipulated emotionally
- Strong and mighty in my thinking
- Peaceful in my heart
- Trusting the outcome will be fine in life or in death
- Grounded in love
- Full and abounding with joy
- Sleeping soundly at night without fear

HEALTHY HEART

If my heart is healthy, my life will be

- Full of hope
- Hearing truth
- Rejecting lies and stupidity
- Tearing down destructive thinking and behaviors
- Emotionally stable
- Steadfast, faithful, and trustworthy
- Working through anxiety, replacing worry with trust
- Quieting myself and learning from others
- Compassionate to those who are hurting.
- Reaching out when I need to be comforted
- Looking for the best in others, but accepting the reality
- Purposefully finding happiness in the little things

- Gentle
- Courageous in the face of fear
- Content
- Calm and peaceful
- Obedient and respectful to authority
- Seeking good counsel
- Subordinate to authority, yet able to lead
- Consistently battling my negative thinking
- Saying: "I am sorry," when I am wrong
- Yielding my right to be right
- Whole-hearted devotion to my recovery
- Denying myself the need to control others

Look into your heart. When your heart is full of strength, courage, hope, love, joy and peace, you can let go of things you can't control nor change. You can let go of the need to be right or the need to have the last word.

What are my motives for being overly involved in another adult's life?

What will it cost me to continue this involvement?

What are the negative emotions I am entertaining today?

| Negative emotions beget negative emotions; like dog begets dog.

Emotions can be useful to warn us to:
- prepare for the traps ahead
- turn and run
- set firm boundaries
- hold others accountable
- seek help for ourselves
- do good deeds.

| Negative emotions, if indulged, are destructive.

Keep a running list of your healthy and destructive emotions today.

If you have no emotions, you may not know how to recognize them. You may have never been validated as a child. You may be very talented at shutting off your emotions. If you are emotionally numb or stuck in the same emotion, seek counseling.

IMMATURE EMOTIONAL TACTICS

List the **immature emotional tactics** used by others you have observed today. If you are at home alone, you can observe the emotional games on news media and television shows.

- Predict who will attempt to use emotional ploys to control and dominate.
- Identify which individuals pacify and sweep issues under the rug.
- Start predicting how characters in your shows (or at work) will respond to a situation. Learn to read people and to discern their motives.
- Find a living example of someone who can handle conflict maturely and bring an issue to resolution.
- Find someone who respects the rights and boundaries of others. These people will make good friends.

How did you do?

Find a dependable person and observe them. Dependable is likely to be solid citizens with emotional stability. These people are boring to enablers who are used to the roller coaster of emotional manipulation. But they are not. They are healthy.

IDENTIFYING A PEACEFUL HOME

I have learned to:

- sing while I wash dishes because I have food.
- cook and serve with a smile.
- think health and strength as I iron the clothes
- never fuss about temporal things.
- practice contentment. (Oh! Now there's a challenge.)
- remember to laugh and enjoy the moment.
- be grateful for laundry because I have clothes.
- think good thoughts while mowing.
- be grateful when I clean the car because I have transportation
- make the bed in gratitude for a night's rest.
- laugh at the silly things in life.
- enjoy dogs wrestling across the floor. (That is a miracle... I used to have no patience for dogs.)

A peaceful home does not just happen. A peaceful home takes practice and responding to life's struggles by growing and maturing.

It is in serving we:

- grow
- develop joy
- become complete

Who can you serve that will not take advantage of you?

Serving persons with abusive behaviors will not bring gratification.
A quiet and patient attitude will honor myself and others.

Describe the home you were raised in:

- How was conflict handled?

- How did we speak to one another?

- Was I bullied, abandoned, mistreated, neglected or abused?

- What behaviors do I want to unlearn?

- What is the goal for my closest relationships?

- What do I need to do to reach my goals?

There is never an excuse to be "unkind".

Think very firm, but patient and kind.

What would it look like if I was quiet, minded my own business, and did my own work?

Practicing manners and common courtesies at home will provide stability and peace. No one can do these things perfectly. This is a daily practice of making moment by moment choices to enjoy a peaceful home.

COPING WITH ANXIETY

CHAPTER 18: DEALING WITH ANXIETY

ANXIETY QUOTIENT QUIZ

(Mark the ones that apply to you)

Anxious
Nervous inside
Snippy – short with others
Impatient
Short term memory loss
Lack of focus
Obsessing over problem – replaying drama
Compulsive speech
Chronic fatigue
Stress with stress induced illnesses
Digestive Problems
Choking on food, water, or your own saliva (swallowing difficulties)
Self-destructive behaviors (cutting, substance abuse)
Jaw clenching
Overreacting (Aggressive)
Under-reacting (Doormat)
Anger (explosive or seething)

Vengeful thoughts, plans or actions
Frequent flus and colds
Impulsive
Ache in back
Frequent crying
Nightmares
Sleep problems
Waking up tormented
Hopeless feeling
Helpless feeling
Despair
Depression (suicidal/homicidal thinking)
Confusion
Fear
Paranoia
Fantasy thinking
Binge eating
Binge television/games
Other dysfunctional self-comforting measures

These are easily identifiable symptoms of anxiety. You may find more.

> There needs to be a decision to stop the anxiety, not to solve the problem. Some of our problems are unsolvable and only acceptance leads to peace.

EMOTIONAL ROLLER COASTER

Crisis– Temporary fix – Temporary Relief – Crisis...

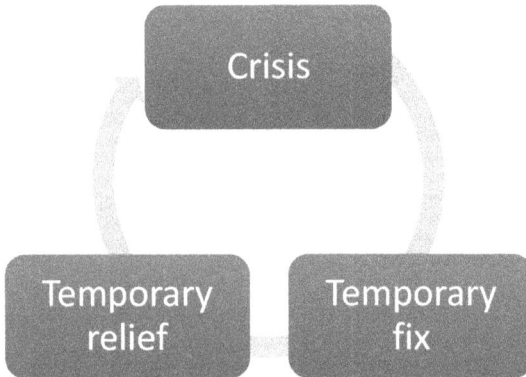

```
         ┌──────────┐
         │  Crisis  │
         └──────────┘

┌──────────┐    ┌──────────┐
│Temporary │    │Temporary │
│  relief  │    │   fix    │
└──────────┘    └──────────┘
```

Stop this roller coaster and let me off.

Powerless over anxiety?

Let's look at the root causes of anxiety:

1. Superficial values (obsessing)
2. Doublemindedness
3. Confusion and chaos
4. Immature emotions
5. Faintheartedness
6. Meditating on drama
7. Taking on someone else's problem
8. Anxiety is a **STOP sign** to slow down and process life
9. Circumstances I cannot control
10. Consequences to poor choices
11. Undisciplined emotional thinking

Be conscience of your symptoms of anxiety. What symptoms of anxiety do you experience?

UNDISCIPLINED THINKING

Anxiety can be as simple as undisciplined thinking

- First, if you purpose to live in the present moment and enjoy it, most anxiety will take care of itself.
- Second, recognize your thoughts.
  - This may require journaling or a trusted friend to find your thoughts.
- Third, reject the thoughts that do not serve you well.
  - Replace them with good thoughts.

Evaluate

Are habitual anxiety patterns ingrained in my brain so deeply that I can't stop the anxiety?

If so, I am stuck and professional counseling is my next step. It should be normal to go to professional counseling when we can't stop our anxiety.

Do I experience deadly symptoms of PTSD, destructive behaviors, suicidal or homicidal thoughts?

If so, this requires immediate counseling and long-term support. Do not let fear hold you back. Empower yourself to overcome any resistance and reach out for help.

> Recognizing anxiety and admitting we are stuck is the biggest step in recovery.

Things to consider

1) Could exercising my "No muscle" relieve anxiety?

2) Is my anxiety intensified by a toxic person?

3) Am I trying to control someone who is out of control?

4) Is there a crazy maker person who takes my power and controls my decisions?

5) Who do I need to distance from my life?

Points to remember

1) The most toxic people I know will not accept boundaries. If a person refuses your "no" boundary, they are not safe. **If you stay in a toxic relationship, you will lose your identity**. Then they will tell you who you are, what to feel, and progressively cut you off from safe people.

2) Abusers isolate you and cut you off from safe people by constantly slandering safe people they cannot manipulate and setting up offenses against them. They have ways to verbally flip circumstances to make themselves look like the victim and entice you to take their side.

3) Find a good friend, a mentor, a support group, or a counselor and plan to distance yourself, or if needed disconnect yourself completely from this person's toxicity.

4) The way you disconnect from toxic person is to die to your emotional connection with them. It is your emotional connection that gives them control over you. Then I want you to become indifferent to an abusive person. I want you to stop listening to their cries and instead send them to other people who they cannot manipulate, but who will hold them accountable.

5) Use your cognition **(conscious mental thinking)** to choose to not let a toxic person have access to your emotional side. This takes practice and a good dose of determination.

6) When you can recognize abuse, you may become very angry.

7) Only superficially indulge this anger, not enough that it owns you. Enough that it empowers you and reinforces your decisiveness to establish boundaries and gives you resolve to escape this person's games.

8) When toxic people can't get an emotional rise out of you, sympathy or financial assistance, you aren't worth their time anymore. They change tactics or go to their next victim to obsess over and torment. But it won't be you!

Refuse anxiety and pursue peace

If there is a disrespectful, contemptuous person in your life, use distance until they choose to respect your boundaries. If that doesn't work, throw them out of your life and demand a change.

Have you made anxiety your best friend?

There is a cure for anxiety.

It is not easy, but simple.

It is a moment by moment choice to refuse anxiety and replace it with gratefulness.

| Don't be anxious about anything, instead, be thankful.

This is a journey. We are learning and growing. Gratefulness changes our focus.

More suggestions

1) Practice enjoying your day moment by moment.
2) Be patient, gentle, but very firm with boundaries.
3) Understand everything in your life is to teach you and make you a better person.
4) Remember to focus on the good things and good people in your life.

| Let peace reign in your heart.
| Turn every anxious thought into a grateful one.

In conclusion, expose any anxiety and its destructive forces and refuse it!!!

| May you have the weapon of gratefulness to guard your peace and protect your heart today!

Start your grateful list here:
I am grateful for:

How do I get off this anxiety train?

There is great suffering:
- until we recognize and admit the dysfunction and make a recovery plan.
- in trying to change people and situations I cannot change.
- when I identify with a broken past.

The key is to detach and let go. Yes, let go! **Wave the white flag of surrender.**

What or who needs surrendered?

In what ways are you your own enemy?

If you are still entertaining anxiety, you are on the enemy's side of the battle. You are tearing down and destroying your own life with anxiety. This behavior plunders you of the enjoyment of your day. It robs you of your health. Anxiety keeps you distracted from things which matter. Anxiety comes with friends of fear, worry, discouragement and confusion.

What you believe about a situation is powerful.

What you say to yourself about a circumstance is powerful.

Reject

- paranoia
- feelings of unworthiness
- helplessness
- restlessness

- fear of the future.

Do not elevate your emotions to the level of truth.

They are just emotions. **Emotions are warning lights on the dashboard of life to show you something in your thinking needs examined, worked through, corrected and released.**

It is your passive thinking that must be reeled in. If you are not purposeful about what you are thinking, anxiety will "own" you and every moment will be filled with anxiety. It is a purposeful identifying and rejecting anxious thoughts that must be done. This takes work! Otherwise, you will be looking for something to distract you from your suffering. Yes, suffering!

Anxiety is a self-induced form of suffering. It is within your power to stop it!

If you are over-responsible, you may lay awake gripped with anxiety. If your loved one in addiction is comfortable and sleeping peacefully in their drunken or drugged stupor, you have way too much of their weight on your shoulders. Give the worry back to them. If they must worry about what to eat, where to sleep, how to pay their bills, or stay out of jail, you can sleep at night because they will be carrying their own self-induced burden. Therefore, place the responsibility of another adult's problems firmly upon their shoulders. This is not your problem, it is theirs.

> **Do not rob them of the chance to mature, grow and experience victory in overcoming their self-imposed burdens of poor decision making. These worries firmly placed on their shoulders might be the very weight they need to correct themselves.**

| Now, rise and claim the peace that is yours.

Here is a place to journal your passive thoughts that come up:
Analyze each passive thought today.
Is it true?

Is it happening now?

Is it my problem?

Are my behaviors helping or hindering my loved one become accountable
and independent?

What thinking do I need to change?

What emotions control you?

Can you feel your countenance change when you indulge anxiety, worry
and fear?

Once you recognize these thoughts clothed in soft garb coming to
manipulate your countenance day after day, you can set up a strategy to
defeat these enemies.

| Recognize the seducing emotions that lure you down the rabbit hole of
stress.

If you have thought about a problem repeatedly for days, weeks or years,
and no solution solves the problem permanently, you can practice

detachment (see chapter 19 on Detachment) from the situation. It is not likely solvable by you.

A choice

It is at this moment a choice.

- Am I going to indulge this anxious attitude, or will I claim my abundant life of peace?
- Am I going to let anxiety make a home with me?
- Or will I declare war and do whatever it takes to get freedom.
- These anxious thoughts are sneaky and subtle. They come and feel as if they are our identity and we naturally react by entertaining their scenarios of destruction.
- These anxious attitudes are unstable and drive us to make foolish decisions that do not serve us well.

I give you permission to denounce anxious, worrisome and fearful thoughts.

Consider

If a thief were at the door, would you let him in? No, of course not! **Every time you indulge anxiety, worry or fear, a thief has entered your house and you will soon be emotionally bound and gagged.** This anxiety will plunder your house. It will snatch your sound mind. Then the loving people who need your time and energy are neglected. They may look for affirmation from others who may ensnare them in a culture of depravity.

| Make no treaty with anxiety.

Declare war!

Get your army (accountability partners) together and arm yourself with courage.

- No surrender
- No retreat.

Just so you know, it usually gets worse before it gets better. When we establish healthy boundaries, toxic people will heat the fire up to another level. They will attempt to push our anxiety and guilt buttons. The goal is to force us to be their marionette puppet again.

Anxiety prepares you to be emotionally manipulated and vulnerable to enable your loved with addiction behaviors, this act of enabling will stop your anxiety, but only temporarily.

Denial is a seductress that lures you with a promise and leaves you empty.

Even after renouncing anxiety, worry and fear, if every few days, there it is again....You need a key to unlock those chains of anxiety.

The key to unlock anxiety is courage. Courage to face life as it come!

What would it look like if I had courage in my life?

Anxiety, worry and fear is me trying to control the wind.

Conquer Anxiety

- I must win the little battles before I can win the war.
- I must choose peace.
- My thoughts must remain in truth and right thinking.

- I must surrender my anxious thoughts.
- I need to denounce and refuse passive thinking.
- Take control over my thought life. This requires me to be in a mental gym.

A mental gym strengthens my correct reasoning and rids me of my flabby thinking.

Now, surrender your flab.

List the things that make you anxious, worrisome or fearful:

If you let go of control, what is the worse that could happen?

What is the best that could happen?

DO MY EMOTIONS RULE?

Emotions are a tricky thing; they will either rule us or we will rule them. Let us identify when our emotions are reigning over us? Ask yourself a few questions:

1. Do I cry often?
2. Am I angry or fearful?
3. Do I feel life is out of control?
4. Do I feel used?
5. Is my life characterized by emotional highs and lows?
6. Do I feel emotionally abused?
7. Do I beat myself up emotionally?
8. Do I feel drained at the end of each day?
9. Do I have depression?
10. Are there losses I have not accepted?
11. Is anxiety high on my list of problems?
12. Do I feel insecure?
13. Does my family have frequent conflict?
14. Does my family ignore or pacify issues to avoid conflict?
15. Is my life characterized by confusion?
16. Do I mull over past or present trauma?

These questions give us lots of fodder for journaling.

Emotions can build fortresses of false thinking and outright lies in our heads.

Find a safe person and talk over these questions.

BUILDING MY OWN IDENTITY

Building my own identity gives me confidence to trust my decisions.

1. Do I permit myself to have a day of rest every week?

2. Can I allow myself to have one frivolous unproductive hour a day?

3. Can I recognize what disturbs my inner peace and refuse it?

4. Can I instruct myself to wait patiently and refuse to fret?

5. Can I be slow to make decisions? Can I be slow to be angry? Can I listen to others?

6. Can I refuse impulsive decisions and make a well thought out plan of action?

7. Can I be quiet inside and confident that all will be well...no matter what?

8. Can I recognize that some people will never have inner peace and that is ok?

9.Can I recognize when I have an imbalance and then get alone to rebalance myself?

10. Can I accept my weaknesses?

11. Can I be kind to myself?

12. Can I keep my heart open and not judge others?

13. Can I protect my heart with a firm boundary without shutting down completely.

14. Can I choose each moment what I will think and will not think?

15. If I stray into a negative thinking trap, how quickly can I recover myself?

16. Can I trust myself to release bitterness and forgive often?

17. Can I find or hope to find another safe person with whom to share life?

18. Can I enjoy being alone?

19. Can I reject manipulative, abusive people without any guilt?

20. Can I have confidence in my abilities to make right choices?

21. Can I address my inner double-talk that brings confusion?

22. Can I let go of my regrets?

23. Can I stop my fretting?

24. Am I free to say no to others? Do I know my limits?

25. Can I stop forcing my way onto others?

26. Can I focus on the good and let go of the bad?

28. Can I reshape the bad and find good in everything?

29. Can I not sweat the small stuff?

30. Do I take care of myself physically, emotionally, mentally, financially and spiritually?

INTENTIONALITY

Do I intend to refuse anxiety and pursue peace?

I must be intentional to recognize my anxiety. Otherwise, half my day is gone before I realize I am obsessing. This may include stressing over a toxic person's irrational words or actions.

Suggested plan

Step 1: Recognize when you are having anxiety?

Step 2: Recognize your body's response to anxiety. Circle your symptoms.

- Racing thoughts
- Confusion or doublemindedness.
- A sense of dread.
- Stomachache.
- Diarrhea/Constipation

- Insomnia
- Eye twitching
- Leg jerking
- Short fuse
- Irritability
- Headaches
- Sore neck
- Elevated shoulders (guarding)
- Muscle spasms

Chronic anxiety

- Gum recession from grinding teeth
- Severe jaw pain from clenching your teeth
- Inflammation and aching joints
- Short term memory loss
- Intense cravings for self-comforting measures used as coping strategies

Step 3: Recognize your triggers. Triggers are people or situations that start my anxiety cycle. Circle the ones that apply.

- Toxic people
- Sweet people with lots of anxiety
- Con artist
- Manipulators
- People with a victim mentality
- Self-pity
- Circumstances that I cannot control
- Events, crowds
- Financial pressures, etc.

Step 4: Develop short and long-term plans to correct your situation.

Meditating on pleasant things gives you the strength to find solutions you never knew were available. Settle yourself and read a good book, learn a new language, play a musical instrument, or focus on a hobby. Join an exercise gym and go to group classes. Volunteer at the Red Cross, soup kitchens, or other places which care for humanity. Find support groups with people working through similar issues: Al-Anon meetings, Celebrate Recovery, etc.

Focus on learning healthy coping skills and not on the anxiety.

Step 5: If you are a praying person, prayer can be a key weapon against anxiety. Not anxious, obsessive prayer, but a trusting child-like faithful prayer. This surrendering to a higher power (however you may understand a higher power) works miracles. This gives us release from carrying the weight of the world on our shoulders.

Step 6: Pursue peace. Take a deep breath and push away anxiety and everything you cannot control and be grateful in all things. **Embrace the diligent, persistent, patient, steadfast character skill of stability you are learning. BE faithful to your own self first.**

Step 7: Purpose to choose courage and enjoy your day. Stay focused and engaged in the present moment.

Irritations

What do I do with all these irritations that could upset my day?

- Running out of gas
- Losing the car keys
- Chronic back injury
- Insomnia
- Chronic joint pain
- Chronic illness/ autoimmune disease

- Immature children throwing fits
- The line at the grocery store is too long
- Stuck in traffic
- A fender bender
- Speeding ticket
- Dog puke (again)
- Burnt dinner
- Demanding boss, co-worker, spouse, parent, or child in my life.

> Whether the irritation is large or small, it doesn't seem to matter. People and circumstances can rob me of the joy of life.

What am I to do with these upsets?

Sometimes, I should mourn with these struggles, but I cannot get stuck in grief. I must grieve and reach out to others to help me through the pain. Often, I need several good friends, so I do not wear one out. Occasionally, isolation can be a short-term antidote to help me process what is really irritating me. Long-term isolation will leave me empty and lonely. **Isolation can also keep me stuck in my head with no one to refute my irrational thinking.**

Minor irritations that are exaggerated into trauma/drama are because of loss of control over other areas of life. This is a dysfunctional attempt to exert control over superficial things.

Freaking out and ranting for an hour over dishes in the sink is indicative of a deeper wound. Overreacting to temporal, superficial situations is because another area of my life is out of control.

Accepting life with all its irritations brings peace.

What would be a mature response to irritations?

What if I took every single irritation and developed more gentleness, patience, kindness and refused to let it rob me of my happiness? Replay your last meltdown. How could you have responded differently?

Use irritations as training

If I feel irritated when:

- in a long line, I let an elderly person or someone with a crying child in front of me.
- stuck in traffic, I meditate on good things, study Spanish words or make an encouraging call.
- I am late or lost, I look for an opportunity to comfort and encourage someone.

Practice flexibility and allow fluctuating circumstances to mold me into a better person.

1) Use every irritation to ponder what you could learn from it. Otherwise,

it seems this life lesson must be repeated.

2) Do not be a hostage in circumstances, but practice loving and patient responses.

3) Let circumstances move and shape your day by learning the **skill of flexibility.**

4) **Let each irritation become an opportunity to hold onto my peace.**

> It seems we receive new opportunities every day to respond to life differently.

How did you do with your irritations today?

The universal law of sowing and reaping follows me.

- **Entertaining anxiety, worry or fear is a magnet for attracting more trouble.**
- **If I choose to respond with love, kindness and patience, my day is good no matter what comes my way.**
- **Pressed down, shaken down, running over... whatever we give, we receive.**

Based upon what you are giving in your relationships, what can you expect to receive?

What are the goals for your closest relationships? Are these goals realistic?

What changes do you need to make in your thinking or actions?

I give you permission to laugh, smile and enjoy a lovely day.

For this is a new day, let us find joy in it.

RECLAIMING YOUR LIFE

CHAPTER 19: DETACHMENT

See short version in Appendix A

PRINCIPLE #1
DETACHMENT IN LOVE WITHOUT FEAR

Detachment is not cold, withdrawn or isolated, but a decision to do what is best for myself first. It is a healthy boundary of knowing where my responsibility begins and where it ends. It is a healthy separation.

I will know when I have done this because I will stop trying to control others and start recognizing my own physical and emotional needs: tired, hungry, angry, lonely, etc.

Practical Steps

1. Step back from the insanity.
2. Leave the room when emotions are high.
3. Do not argue or talk with someone who isn't sober.
4. Refuse to be provoked.
5. Do not take abusive words as truth or internalize them.
6. When it is the other person's emotional pain, let them own it.
7. Allow yourself to identify and feel all your emotions. Move through emotions quickly. (This is an **emotional maturity skill** that must be cultivated.)

8. Do not think of yourself as an emotion, but as stability. An example is fear vs. courage.
9. Understand **most people will not change without suffering.** Suffering, for some, can be a good motivator for change. They need it. Do not rescue them from consequences of poor choices.
10. A person making absurd decisions may need the consequences of their choices to change their behaviors.

PRINCIPLE #2
DETACHMENT BRINGS PEACE

Detachment is not caring less but caring more for my emotional stability. Ask yourself some questions:

- Is it my problem?
- Is it my responsibility?
- Is it a consequence to a poor choice?
- Is it a consequence of defiance, rebellion or breaking the law?
- Who are my emotionally, unbiased counselors?
- Is this person exhibiting self-destructive behaviors that have deep roots?
- Are there children who need nurtured or protected?

Am I enmeshed? The definition of **Enmeshment** is to be entangled or wrapped up in a net. (See Entanglement Gauge)

Can I experience freedom to be happy when others are depressed?

Does my inner peace depend upon another person's sobriety?

PRINCIPLE #3
DETACHMENT IS FINDING HEALTHY IDENTITY

My emotional stability is not dependent on another person or their sobriety.

What do I do when the world is crashing around me with addiction issues?

- Separate myself emotionally and physically.
- Build myself up with healthy relationships. Understand that staying in toxic relationships means I am emotionally sick.
- Things usually get worse before they get better. Understand if I interrupt recovery in a person with substance use disorder with enabling, they will likely relapse.
- Practice the higher levels of Love. (See chapter 16 on Love)
- Look for true repentance (See "True and False Repentance")
- Have compassion and make a difference if you can. Research to find good counselors, recovery centers or support groups you and your loved one could attend. You lead the way and get help for yourself.

    Almost every individual with addictive behaviors has an enabler who is also sick. Individuals caught in any addiction need more help than an enabler can give them.

- In what or whom is my identity? Is it in a higher power, my political influence, personal power, or money?
- Am I in constant anxiety? Can I learn to feel my emotions and let them go?
- Do I refuse to be emotionally manipulated?
- Can I quiet my fears?

- Do I think I have the power to change my loved one?
- Am I pulling them out of the fire or am I being pulled in?
- Am I addicted to rescuing my loved one with an addictive behavior?
- What am I doing that perpetuates the addictive cycle?
    - Excuse making
    - Interrupting consequences
    - Not requiring accountability
    - Not requiring them to work or pay their own fees/fines.

PRINCIPLE #4
DETACHMENT RESPECTS BOUNDARIES

- Can I let others make their own choices and have their own consequences without suffering?
- Can I say no with love and not hatred?
- Can I say no without fear and anxiety?
- Can I respect another when they say no?
- Can I see my own manipulative behaviors?
- Can I choose what I will and will not tolerate?
- Can I follow through with my choices?
- Have I built rigid and isolating walls that make me lonely?
- Have I built strong boundaries with movement which can be changeable and moveable if needed?
- Do my responses and actions encourage personal growth, connectedness, and maturity?
- Do I focus on what I cannot change or on what I can change?
- Am I consumed with worries about the future?
- Can I have the courage to face "one day at a time"?

PRINCIPLE #5
DETACHMENT MEANS, "MINDING MY OWN BUSINESS"

- Can I see my unhealthy behaviors? Can I refuse drama?
- Can I see my own emotional baggage?
- Do I choose to work on making myself healthier?
- Do I gossip? Am I a nagger?
- Do I slander or rail another?
- Do I induce problems to manipulate or control others?
- Am I harboring bitterness, resentments or un-forgiveness that needs to be addressed?
  Practical Tips: Have I:
  - made my bed?
  - taken out my trash?
  - cleaned up my yard?

If I **mind my own business**, I can have the energy to care for myself and address my character flaws and position myself with others who can mentor, encourage, and hold me accountable for my actions.

- Am I practicing quiet reflective thinking?
- Can I quiet my fears?
- Can I quiet my mind?
- Can I prioritize my daily routine?
- Can I manage my time?
- Am I paralyzed because of negative emotions?
- Do I make quick and foolish decisions?
- Which negative emotion(s) controls me?
  - Anger

- Bitterness
- Fear
- Fretting and Anxiety
- Depression

Unmet Needs

When I have unmet needs, what negative behaviors do I exhibit to comfort myself?

- Mind altering substances (even prescription medications)
- Alcohol, excessive sugar, or overeating
- Sexually acting out
- Suicidal/homicidal/angry/bitter thoughts
- Compulsive shopping or gambling, television, etc.
- Obsessive thinking
  - Can I acknowledge my unmet needs?
  - Can I ask for what I need?
  - Do I know how to reach out to others?
  - Can I take care of myself and my needs first?

PRINCIPLE #6
DETACHMENT MEANS FORGIVENESS

Be kind and forgive.

- If we do not forgive, we cannot find forgiveness.
- Indulging bitterness robs, defiles, and troubles us.
- If we do not forgive, we will be the one who is tormented.
- However, if we accept suffering and forgive our offender this releases

us and brings us emotional stability.

How do I forgive when I do not feel like it?

1. Forgiveness is the right thing to do.
2. Forgiveness does not pardon the offender from consequences.
3. Forgiveness is for my benefit.
4. Forgiveness is not forgetfulness. It needs a strong boundary until trust is earned.
   - Realize suffering is a part of this world.
   - Let your suffering make your heart tender to make you a protector of innocent children.
   - Use suffering to help you make choices to change, so your future looks different than your past.
   - List the good things that have come from your suffering.
   - Get a vision and a goal. Where do you want to be in a month, a year, and in five years?

Truth

Healing comes when we go to others who can help us stop the enabling addiction cycle and accept beneficial counsel.

- Only you have the power to stop the agony of enabling in your life.
- Let the past go.
- Move forward.

PRINCIPLE #7
DETACHMENT MEANS THINKING DIFFERENTLY

- What do you think about yourself?
- Whose voice is in your head rejecting you?

- Is there a past trauma event that identifies who you are today?
  - Find a refuge. A quiet place to claim what is yours with kindness and firmness.
  - **This addiction battle does not belong to me. I cannot win sobriety for another.**
  - My victory is secured by exercising my right to say NO with firmness and kindness.
    Courage is the secret to overcoming enabling behaviors.

PRINCIPLE #8
DETACHMENT MEANS AVOID THE WHIRLWIND

Rules of survival

- If a man does not work, he shouldn't eat.
- Make no friendship with stupidity.
- Withdraw yourself from confusion and disorder.
- **Have nothing to do with an angry person.** Do not engage them until they have control over their emotions. **Walk away!**
- Warn a person once, warn them twice and have nothing to do with him. **My sanity is too important to indulge immature emotions and behaviors.** Most likely you have warned them a hundred times. They are not listening.

PRINCIPLE #9
DETACHMENT MEANS TO BEAR A PERSON'S CRISIS BUT LET HIM CARRY HIS OWN LOAD

Crisis

- Accident, tragedy, natural disaster, severe illness or a major loss.

Personal Load

- Let others climb their own mountains, so they may become strong.
- Let them be responsible to pay their utilities, car insurance, car payment, gas or food.

   We are considering one who has squandered their provisions on cigarettes, movies, drugs, alcohol, gambling, or frivolous shopping and eating out. We are not talking about the working poor, or ill.

   - In this case, you may want to take your loved one to a financial course and teach them to manage their money.
   - It is important to let them learn quick and early to carry their own personal load or their financial struggles will snowball.
      - **If we become a pushover for the irresponsible, we will reap the consequences.**
      - **If I am over-responsible, it will allow others to be under-responsible.**

PRINCIPLE #10
DETACHMENT MEANS TO LEARN FROM MY MISTAKES

- Brokenness over past mistakes is not wailing and wallowing in despair.
- It is not brooding or beating myself up.
- It is not self-destructive behaviors.
- Brokenness is a death of my expectations.
- A coming to an end of myself and releasing all my wishes and desires and letting go of what I cannot control.
- It is an acceptance of the inability to change others.

PRINCIPLE #11
DETACHMENT MEANS SEPARATING MYSELF FROM THE PROBLEM

- This is easy, but not simple.
- Immaturity soaks up the emotions of others around us and mirrors them back.
- Can I recognize and stop my obsessing?
- Maturity recognizes the emotion and feels it intensely and then releases it.
- Ruling my own emotions is the key to enjoying my day. It is a shutting out the negativity around me.
- It is a refusing to think on, act on, or get involved in things that are none of my business.
- There is a separation from adult children. A launching them into

independent living to care for themselves and to solve their own problems.

- I may counsel and give advice.
- I may do research and help them look at options.
- I must see the problem outside of me. I am not their savior.
- I may make deadlines and gradually add more boundaries and give the adult child more responsibilities.

Coddling leads to a life of suffering and dependency.

PRINCIPLE #12
DETACHMENT MEANS I CAN ENJOY MY DAY

Detachment is not abandonment, but love. It is making decisions without emotions and choosing to enjoy my day.

Unhealthy ways of caring

- Rescuing
- Coercing
- Manipulating
- Taking charge of dysfunctional adults
- Paying their bills
- Rescuing from consequences
- Making excuses
- Overreacting
- Demanding
- Controlling

Healthy ways of caring

- Choosing what is best for me.
- Boundaries against the immature or abusive.
- Holding others accountable for thefts.
- Calling them out on their lies.
- Giving your loved one direction on where to receive help.
- Leave the decision for recovery in the hands of your loved one.
- Distance myself from anyone with active addictive behaviors.
- Protect my heart by loving them with my head and not my emotions

The greatest detachment skill I have learned is to "die to my emotions".

If I am dead (detached) to my emotions, I cannot be manipulated emotionally. I can make decisions that are rational, thought out and purposeful. Do not be an emotional puppet or an easy target for the financial extortion of a person with addictive behaviors.

All addiction behaviors whether they are drugs, alcohol, gambling, food, workaholics, enabling, television, games, or any other self-indulgent comforting is rooted in a wound and unmet needs. Recovery explores these issues deep within our souls and helps us plan for lasting change. **All addictive behaviors are destructive and cause suffering.**

- A **calloused heart** is stuck in pain, refuses change, and stays in a vicious cycle.
- A **surrendered heart** is totally releasing others, working on me and producing a "Free Spirit".
- <u>**Free to enjoy my life, no matter what!!!**</u>

***Learn to find the good in great times of sorrow.

Destructive Behavior Patterns

When destructive behavior patterns cannot be broken:

- **Stop**
- **Acknowledge negative thinking**
- **Surrender what cannot be changed**
- Practice quietness inside and pursue contentment

CHAPTER 20: WHO IS HINDERING YOU?

Do not turn away from freedom and go back into the cycle of enabling!

When you are facing those who are selfish and have set themselves up as their own authority and will not listen to anyone, here is some things to ponder:

1) There are people who pervert truth to their own advantage, and they are good at it. **Reject their nonsense.**

2) Deceitful people can be so convincing because they have even deceived themselves. **Recognize the lies.**

3) Do not stay in the presence of rebellious people and **do not let them trap you emotionally or financially**. Often, individuals with addictive or abusive behaviors can pretend to be extremely kind. But say, NO to them and see if they respect your NO or if they flip personalities and become depraved and incorrigible. If so, the "real" person beneath the cloak of pretense has just been unveiled.

Ask yourself

1) Am I being charmed and corrupted away from stability?

2) Am I putting up with people who are placing me under their thumb and telling me what to do?

3) Are they pretending that everything they do is right and

refusing counsel?

4) Do they have me in bondage emotionally, physically and financially?

5) Has my peace been devoured?

6) Has my freedom been hampered?

7) Do they run recklessly down the road with no thought to the consequences?

8) Are they taking my money, time, and energy?

9) Am I assuming their responsibilities?

10) If I confront them, do they hit me physically or bully me with words or double talk?

Now let us look for some suggestions when handling people who pervert my life.

4) In trying to please the unpleasable people in my life, I have forgotten to be true to myself.

Think of this perverter as the television, the manipulator, the abusers, or the bullies in your life. These people twist truth and coerce you with fear. They could be in your schools, communities, churches, or even in your home. Speaking their great swelling words repeatedly until they believe their own lies and bully others. This continues until you go along with them.

5) Those that use perversion of truth are masters at manipulation.

6) We cannot find balance in chaos. Turn off the chaos. Get alone, get quiet, and find your own way. In cases of addiction, many enablers are being shoved into the path of a speeding train of destruction. After ten or twenty years of rescue attempts... you have only one viable choice, **save yourself and let them go**. They do not want to be responsible and change. In fact, they do not need to if they are continually bailed out of consequences. Your courage to change may be their only hope.

Ask yourself

- Who am I trying to please?
- Is someone trying to make me obsessed with their needs at my expense?
- Have I been bewitched (controlled), entangled, or enticed?
- Am I trying to fix someone by bribing them for good behavior?
- Do I think money is all I need to solve problems?

When we have freed ourselves, <u>do not</u> forget the chronic days, weeks, and years of abuse. Do not turn away from freedom and go back into the cycle of enabling!

1) How have people with addictive or abusive behaviors affected me?
2) What burdens have been put on me?
3) What burdens have I accepted and put on myself that was not mine?
4) How has my daily peace been hindered?
5) Those causing trouble need to bear their own consequences and they should.
6) When I set up boundaries and am no longer accessible to manipulate, they may change or have no use for me and leave me alone.

It is ok if an individual with addiction behaviors separates themselves from us! This usually comes with great trauma when we are placing healthy boundaries.

Expect it. Die (detach) emotionally to a sick relationship, so we cannot be emotionally manipulated. They will return as a victim when their next enabler turns them out. Make them earn the right to be trusted by showing a good work ethic and making restitutions for their wrongs. Do not accept a "hard luck" story. If they are so unstable that suicide is imminent, get immediate counsel!

7) Remember the law of sowing and reaping and do not interrupt their reaping of consequences or they will not learn.
8) If they sow to the wind, let them reap the whirlwind.
9) Do not stick your head in the sand and think problems will go away. Instead, work on things that are within your control to change. You can only change you!

Hold onto your freedom to regain control over your own life. Do not get entangled again.

Hold your head high and speak no dirty words.

Stick to your beliefs in the simplicity of hard work and responsibility.
So, do you recognize those with impure motives?

Do you love a person who refuses to take responsibility for their actions?

Who is hindering you and keeping you emotionally unstable?

Are you hindering another? Go and apologize quickly.

It may take a few weeks or months but plan to thoughtfully untangle yourself.

Apology

Now to you who are suffering from the emotional pain of abuse, I apologize. I am sorry for your suffering. I apologize to you for everyone who has ever hurt you and are unable or unwilling to repent. I give you permission to release your offender from the debt they owe you. I set you free. Take a deep breath and exhale and let go. This is a new day. May you be free to be the person you were created to be.

CHAPTER 21: DON'T BE FOOLED BY THE DEVOURER

AKA relationship addictions

This lesson is for the enablers who want free from an abusive relationship. If you recognize the cycle of a dysfunctional relationship, you will not end up in the same place again. Anytime you meet someone and there is intense passion distance yourself until you have observed their behavior and investigated their past relationship history with others. Usually with a little resistance from you, they will be distracted to an easier prey and you will escape their snare.

4 Phases of a Devourer

1) Intense Passion
2) Rollercoaster
3) Trauma/Drama
4) Chewed up and spit out

Intense Passion: Addicted to Love

- A consuming and exciting relationship
- You become the center of the world
- Feel valued and loved and needed

- Lots of affection and intensity
- You become the answer to their emptiness

> Reality: You are their latest obsession. They are in love with the idea of being in love, but not with you.

- Appearances are important
- Lust is strong; it feels like devotion and true love
- They are intensely gratified with you.
- You are set up as their savior
- The answer to their chasm of emptiness
- Long talks
- Multiple daily texts and/or calls
- Your time is being consumed
- Other relationships are pushed aside
- You start to **lose your identity** and are molded into a new one

Roller Coaster (Manipulation Begins)

- Discontent sets in
- Mood swings
- His/her ways are moveable
- You feel like you are trying to hold the wind
- Whatever pleased them yesterday, angers them today.
- Intense emotional highs/lows
- You begin the role of the "pleaser".
- You start to lose your own identity.
- Your responsibility is to make them happy.
- Keeping them emotionally stable is a full-time job.
- Their eyes are at the end of the world.

- o I want...
- o Give me...
- o If you really cared... A shower of satisfaction and gratefulness comes when they achieve what they want. Until, they want the next thing.
- o Cycle repeats (it usually intensifies... demands are greater)
- o Usually there is a new hoop to jump through every day or even every hour.
- o Whether they rage or laugh there is no peace.
- o The nagging and whining returns
- o I want...
- o I need...
- o Only if...
- o A continual replay of old wounds...
- o And disappointments of old relationships rehashed....
- o The agitation begins verbally and mounts until they can justify their position... sometimes the position is an act of violence/theft (cleaning out your bank account) or other violation towards you. Recognize the cycle.

Trauma/Drama-The Game Heats Up

- Eventually, no matter what you do, it is not good enough.
- Pushing buttons.
- Unreasonable demands.
- Just to see if you will play the "love game", because of course any boundary or NO is evil and **not** respected.
- Comparison is made to an imaginary perfect relationship.
- Turning your words against you.
- Bringing up your past.

- Self-pity, tears.
- Depression.
- Intense anger in them and/or in you.

Chewed up and Spit Out

- Confusion
- Blaming
- Name calling
- Withdraw
- Silent treatment
- Obsessing
- They live in fantasy and not reality (men may indulge in pornography, women, most often, indulge in soft porn: romance movies or novels, or soap opera type television).
- Then, they feel ashamed, guilty or at the very least distracted from reality.
- Next, they twist it to make their depression or anger your fault or your responsibility.
- They attempt to control every aspect of your life:
- **Instigation stage**: This stage is important because it pushes you over the edge. They blame you for the relationship failure. This allows them to continue being the victim and shun any possible responsibility.

If you retreat

- You will **lose your identity**
- Walk on eggshells
- Think it is all your fault
- Blame yourself and beat yourself up

- Try harder
- You become emotionally unstable as they convince you every day... "You are crazy!"
- You doubt your intuition because they tell you your perceptions are wrong.
- If you start to figure things out, they switch game plans.
- You feel like their pet.
- Your goal is to return to the passion phase of "true love", but that was their pseudo-reality to get you on the hook and not within your ability to recover.

At this point, the relationship has not met their fantasy and needs to be destroyed.

The relationship failure must be securely fixed on you, so they can justify a clear conscience and of course, play the victim for their next prey.
Once they are done with you or you set up even the smallest boundary:
- They play helpless in distress and emotionally devastated.
- They look for their next victim.
- They push through every boundary.
- If you are not controllable, they are upset.
- Their warped view of love is "control".
- But if you are controllable, they lose respect for you.
- You are rejected. It is a no-win situation....

Other symptoms of a "Devourer" relationship

- Passive/Aggressive
- Anger and dominance

- Cyclical patterns of dysfunctional thinking and behaviors
- **Bone throwing** is where they pretend to return to the passion phase. This keeps you on the hook, while they look for the new lover.

Understand: They are completely incapable of loving you!

Why can't they love you?

- They are enamored with themselves and possibly adorned in fine clothes to hide their insecurities.
- They look at themselves often in a mirror.
- Emotionally immature.
- They are incomplete as a person. They have a divided heart and soul.
- They are double-minded and unstable in all their ways.

Potentially you can still be valuable to them. They will think of a new plot and set up strategies to suck you in emotionally. The lure used is recapturing the intensity of the relationship enjoyed at the beginning. When you take the bait and they get what they want, you are once again abused and discarded.

Then the elaborate plan begins it is all your fault. After all, accepting responsibilities or respecting your boundaries is not even visible skill on their radar.

Identifying a Devourer

Here are some potential behaviors to help you identify a devourer:

- Vanity.
- Searching for compliments.
- Heart of a hunter/pursuer.
- Never satisfied or content.

- Unable to ever love you, because they love themselves too much.
- Frequent pity parties; moody.
- Emotional intensity alternating with instability.
- Manipulating master.
- Refuses to accept responsibility.
- String of past broken relationships.
  - Excuse making.
  - Intense/consuming/passion.
  - Control freaks.
  - Lack of respect for others.
  - Surrounded by others who tell them what they want to hear.
  - A real actor/actress.
  - Flirtatious.
  - Attention seeking.

Too Good to Be True

At the beginning, they play a role too good to be true:

- Beware of Lust.
- Lust drives intense emotions.
- Intense lust can be a sister to explosive anger.
- Watch for road rage when they are driving.
- Verbalization of excuse making, blaming and anger against authority figures: parents, teachers, employers, police, etc.

EMOTIONAL IDENTIFIERS OF A DEVOURER

- Whining.
- Complaining.

- Demanding.
- Withdrawing.
- Unappeasable.
- Talks negatively about old lovers.
- Obsessive thinking.
- Daydreaming.
- Fantasy-vacation exploits.
- Replays past offenses.
- Guilt and shame drive them from reality.
- They make up their own reality.
- Lack responsibility to identify and work on their own issues.
- Everything is someone else's fault.
- Seek lots of sympathy.

HOW TO ESCAPE A DEVOURER

- Work on your own emotional maturity.
- Recognize intense lust creates dysfunctional relationships.
- Recognize your passive/aggressive behaviors.
- Surround yourself with accountability.
- Face your past, so, your future can look different.
- Stop denying.
- Find safe people.
- Ask accountability partners to expose your blind spots.
- Find a servant's heart (not with the person you are addicted to, but with those near your circle of influence: elderly parents, children, co-workers, friends, handicapped or elderly neighbors.).

WORK A RECOVERY PROGRAM

- Find safe relationships worth investing in.
- Realize if you have become like the devourer.
- Understand how your relationship failures repeat themselves.
- Recognize any over-reacting emotionally to situations as a signal to deal with your unhealed wounds.
- Work on becoming a whole person.
- Develop your own identity.
- Attend a love and sex recovery meeting and just listen.
- Real relationships are not fairytales, they are work.

Is there any hope for a marriage like this?

It is helpful to recognize these behaviors, so you can detach from your emotions and stop the manipulation and dominance over you. Healthy boundaries are often met with the other person ending the relationship. But at least you know, it was all a game.

If the person truly comes to responsibility, submits to counseling, accountability partners, and consistently works a recovery program to heal their past wounds, it is possible for them to recover. But it is a lot of work. Underneath these behaviors is a very wounded person. They must recognize their dysfunction and determine to heal and change. Only they can make those decisions. The best thing you can do is to work your own recovery and accountability program. This will either propel the other person into a recovery program or will cause the situation to escalate.

Remember

- You can only control yourself.
- Attempting to control others will drive you crazy.
- If the relationship is violent or destructive, it is time to get good counsel and step back physically and emotionally so you can determine what is best for

you.

- Addictive relationships will not usually start to recover without a crisis.
- The crisis can be good. It can force you to look at reality and make a plan that looks different for your future.
- If you stay in an addictive relationship pattern, you will not like who you become.
- Addictions never bring health or healing.

FINAL THOUGHTS

CHAPTER 22: BRIDGE BUILDING WITH ONE IN RECOVERY

Talk is cheap. Action speaks volumes.

Evaluation Questions

1. Are they truly repentant or just sorry for the consequences?
2. Do they have a short and long-term plan for recovery?
3. Are they dealing with the real problems or just the consequences?
4. Do they have an accountability partner or a recovery group?
5. Are they willingly under authority: courts, family, employment, school, etc.?
6. Have they acknowledged full responsibility for their poor choices?
7. Who received the last financial consequence you or your loved one with SUD?
8. Are they hiding anything?
9. Are they developing accountability groups and a support team?
10. Are they choosing healthy friends?
11. Are they making restitution for past offenses?
12. Do they respect your boundaries?
13. Are they serving others and giving back to the family and community?
14. Do they consistently repeat a cycle of regret/relapse? If so, they need stronger boundaries and/or harder consequences.

Recovery Behaviors

Other positive behaviors indicative of recovery

- Building relationships where there is mutual sharing and support.
- Grieving after relapse and voluntarily setting up stronger accountability.
- Willingly submits to drug screens.

Recovery Suggestions

- You may want to use a third party to rebuild the relationship.
- Anger management skills may be necessary.
- Money management skills may be necessary.
- Someone monitoring the situation who is not sympathetic with the person with SUD.
- Someone who is authoritarian enough to hold them accountable with tough consequences.

> When it comes to recovery, do not expect perfection but do require progress.

There may be a period that you cannot emotionally handle seeing them suffer. Most of our enabling behaviors are because we suffer for our loved ones. This may necessitate a time to allow them to grow and mature and make healthy choices without you. Protect your recovery. Work a plan to not enable others to stay on a destructive path. Enabling can cause a quick slide into relapse. It takes great courage to take a step back from our controlling and manipulating. As a recovering enabler, we need someone to monitor all of our decisions regarding our loved one with addictive behaviors and our relationship with them.

Recovery Accountability

- Keeping our financial accounts open to the scrutiny of another who understands enabling addictions.
- Keeping all your phone calls with your loved one with SUD and co-enablers on speaker phone for others to hold you accountable to not enable.
- Keeping all your visits short and with a trusted friend or companion with you.
- No physical or verbal contact for a specified period may be needed.
- Possibly letter writing for 30 days to a year may be appropriate.

Walk in your recovery one day at a time. Understand your addiction to rescue your loved one with SUD is destructive. Understand enablers are the center of the problem that empowers the addiction cycle. Speak truth in love. Make others earn your trust. This needs to be at least a two-year journey. Do not tolerate any anger, or manipulation towards you.

Have courage and trust your loved one to find their own path in life.

PROTECT THE INNOCENT

If you are a parent/spouse of an individual with active substance use disorder or other destructive addiction behaviors and you have other children or you have their children, do not allow them access to the children unless legally required to do so.

Not only is the manipulation and stubbornness contagious, but the younger child may also be grieved over the person's behaviors and not understand the addiction issues. They may think that if they can identify with the person with substance use disorder and love him more, they could help him. The innocent child or sibling may attempt to become like this person in areas of depression or suicidal tendencies in an attempt to connect with them.

If the child or younger sibling observes the person overdose and be resuscitated, it may leave a lifetime trauma. It will take much counseling before the innocent child or younger sibling can overcome their fears and anxieties. They may need professional counseling to address the lies they believe before they can stop grieving for the family member caught in addictive behaviors.

If you have younger children in the home, carefully consider the sacrifice you may be making to allow persons in active addiction access to you, your home, or these innocent ones. I would require one to two years of progressive recovery and then only supervised, structured visits.

Also, if a younger child exhibits anxiety, depression or starts to cut themselves, let go of the adult with chronic addictive behaviors and focus on the younger child and possibly you can avert a tragedy of having two children in the family in addiction.

CHAPTER 23: NINETY-NINE DEATHS: MOURNING THE LOSS

Don't try to bear this sorrow alone.

Some loved ones with SUD reap the consequences of their poor choices quickly and overdose and die within days, weeks, or months of their first use. These are great tragedies. Your loved one did not even have a chance to turn their life around. My heart goes out to you and I am sorry for your great loss. Find grief support groups and mourn with others.

Other enablers have loved ones who have addiction behaviors that started at a young age and may have other behavioral health issues and a perplexing cycle of confusion. Ask yourself:

- Were they given drugs or alcohol by a parent or sitter as a toddler in their baby bottle?
- Was the mother addicted and the child exposed to alcohol or drugs in the womb?
- Do they come from a long line of alcoholics and have a genetic predisposition to addictive behaviors?

If the substance use disorder characteristics start at a young age and the behaviors become part of their personality, they may be facing a life-long addiction. Young people with addictive behaviors **need us** to toughen up and intervene swiftly with stern and painful consequences. Before they are 18 (age limits are younger in some states), you can choose their rehabilitation plan. Don't coddle them or you may be facing a lifetime of suffering and destruction. Spend your money on treatment, counseling, and random drug screens, and accountability. It will be worth it to evade the tragic suffering awaiting an individual caught in a life-long addiction cycle. Otherwise, assuming they do not die quickly, you could possibly be facing ninety-nine episodes of life-threatening impending doom. A death that never ends.

> Addiction is a death that never stops coming and suffering that never ends.

Severe behavioral health disorders may not respond to treatment or even worsen with treatment. The attempt to alleviate behavioral health disorders can be impossible when coupled with severe addiction. The addiction may drive the person to consume a month supply of six different prescription medications in a few days. This type of substance use can cause heart, kidney, and liver issues and certainly brain damage. When your loved one comes off of a seven-day drug or alcohol binge, raging and violence are imminent, and they are at great risk for suicide. Call the police and have them incarcerated where they are safe from themselves. Work with the courts to confine them in a court ordered treatment center where they can find sobriety. When their mental faculties are clear, possibly they can choose a different path in life.

If you have tried to help for a decade, you are not helping. After 7-10 treatment centers and multiple failed out-patient recovery programs, they are not doing the work to recover. Distance yourself from them. Nice clothes and nice cars only establish their credentials to entice unsuspecting new enablers. Then you may have sorrow upon sorrow: multiple overdoses, abortions, abandoned children, beaten partners, and imprisonments.

> Expect to be considered an enemy when you refuse to rescue them from consequences.

They will likely turn every new enabler against you, so you cannot warn them. They will divide you from other co-enablers and you may lose many relationships. This will compound your suffering as you watch new enablers get reeled in hook, line and sinker and elderly enablers go bankrupt and lose their home.

While you die emotionally to them a little more every year, you may find yourself crying … a lot. My suggestion is to mourn and detach emotionally to them. This way you can never be emotionally manipulated. This death is a death that will continue 10 times, 20 times even 99 times.

> You must grieve and let go and grieve and let go again and again.

When you think you cannot mourn anymore something will happen to open your heart and you may become sympathetic again and will have to grieve again. Harden your heart towards them and guard your heart from this insanity. This is a survival choice for you.

You are not going to change them. It is only you that you have the power to change. Once you start to detach, you will mourn. Do not let yourself grieve more than 5 minutes at a time. Discipline yourself to stop and redirect your focus. You cannot cry a river daily for a decade; you won't survive. Even with all this self-induced suffering, you are still powerless over another person's addictive behaviors. Now, take a deep breath and release your loved one to your higher power.

Realize the facts

While you are suffering and grieving and lying awake at night fretting, they are partying and dealing drugs to get drugs and beating their new enablers and running up stolen credit cards and maybe even molesting children and manipulating everything and everyone in their path to get more drugs. Write down all unacceptable behaviors, so you may **slay the dragon of sympathy that drives your enabling**. When this person pretends to be helpless, remember those facts.

> Detach a little more each day to them and live a little more each day for you.

Know that this is a journey of a thousand tears. Understand that even if you shed a million tears, you cannot change or control another person's decisions or the outcome of their lives. Breathe and release your pain and find healing for yourself and learn to love another who can genuinely love you back.

> Visualize my heart reaching out to yours to send you love and peace.

CHAPTER 24: REFLECTIVE QUIET MOMENTS

Trust others to find their own way!

These are some of my reflections I hope you enjoy them and can start journaling your own thoughts for recovery.

What is the greatest cause of anxiety?

Could it be an attempt to control the uncontrollable? Today, say to yourself a hundred times, "I am loved." When I first did this, it made me weep. I know I am loved, but I did not hold sacred the love I knew others had for me and myself for them. I did not love myself. I did not trust things would work out without my anxious controlling of people and circumstances. I did not trust others to find their own way.

Instead, I wandered in paranoia and rejected love. When love comes from others, I reject it because of my feelings of unworthiness or my restless heart. I expect it to be false and followed by manipulative behaviors and coercion. When I don't heal my emotional wounds of neglect, abandonment, or abuse, it is difficult to trust or to begin healthy relationships. I am always assuming others are selfish and self-serving, and I wait for them to hook me in for continual drama and abuse.

Can I identify the people who are safe in my life?

I rejected love and its' accompanying peace and chose to walk in anxiety.

The Great Lie

**Anxiety became such a familiar companion
that I thought the anxiety was me!**

This lie set up a stronghold and I was BOUND in CHAINS.

While daily walking in anxiety, I forgot the power that lives within me. I forgot I could stir up love through quiet prayer and simple trust. I felt my love was scattered and feeble and I would hide myself from people who could love me. And I would give myself to those who dominated and controlled me. (Just like anxiety dominates.)

Anxiety shrouds me in DARKNESS and robs me of healthy relationships and set me on a path of loneliness and depression.

Maybe I am attempting to repeat my past and find a better solution. But that is not possible. It would just be a different face with a different name at a different place. It takes emotional maturity to choose healthy relationships.

Peace is Mine through Quiet Meditation

But peace is mine. It belongs to me. Why do I not know this peace?

Could it be that I have laid down my greatest weapon?

Could it be my weapon was stolen by circumstances?

Could my anxiety have convinced me of the vanity of quiet reflective meditation?

Has the noise in my head and daily distractions in my life become obstacles between me and my inner peace?

Elevating anxiety is the wrong side

Anxiety is on the side of the enemy!!!

Now refuse anxiety!

Rise up and claim what is yours!

Seek pure love with a fierceness of the warrior you were created to be.

Claim peace that is greater than your circumstances.

Do not be anxious

May you be empowered through a child-like trust to conquer your anxiety and place yourself on the right side of the battle. This walk of faith is not passive. It is strong and bold with great courage. It refuses lies and manipulation. It can choose between right and wrong with mental soundness. It can observe the burdens of life with contentment. It can let go of what I cannot change yet change everything I can. **Faith brings mental clarity** of purpose and not confusion. Peace and not chaos. Enjoyment of each moment.

Describe the thing that hinders you from experiencing this quiet, trusting heart.

What is your deepest disappointment?

Do you feel mentally and emotionally strong?

Joy is my birthright.

How can I find joy?

First, I must stop my grieving over the past.

This is a purposeful choosing to let go of sorrow and weeping.

I must recognize fretting and stop.

I must purpose to forgive others and myself.

Let others live their lives however they choose.

Yet, at the same time, I must give myself permission to choose to live my life in joy.

What is the secret to finding this inner strength?

Quietness (in my thoughts) and confidence (in my heart) shall be my strength.

My friend, no matter how much suffering and hardship you have experienced, listen to these words, quiet your anxious thoughts, strengthen yourself, and choose joy each moment. Now, take a deep breath.

I give you permission to "let go" of the past and enjoy your day.

Where is my peace?

Where is my peace?

How can it so easily elude me?

I know it is a gift, so does it come in a box?

How does it get away so quickly?

Does it have legs to run on?

Does it hide behind my problem or under the bed?

How can it be so near, yet be oh so very far?

How can it be so hard to find, but oh so easy to lose?

.... seek peace and pursue it.

What am I pursuing today?

How do I develop an inner peace?

Be still, ...

This is not an option; it is a command I give you.

What would it look like to be still?

Would it be a disciplined mind to think only true, honest, and accurate thoughts.

Reject all negative nonsense and chaos.

What thoughts would you think?

What words would I say?

Let the words of my mouth, and the meditation of my heart, be lovely and hopeful….

The words of my mouth will match the thoughts in my heart.

So, when I struggle, I must correct my thinking first in order to gain control over my speech.

There is an old proverb that says: For as a man thinks in his heart, so is he...

...for out of the abundance of the heart his mouth speaks.

Be careful what you allow near your heart.

Every idle word I speak comes back to me. Whether it is good or bad.

I need some strong tape to slow down my mouth, until I can get my thinking straight and my heart in tune.

What has been your ditch this week?

It is our mind and emotions which needs regenerated by daily choosing right thinking. We do not have to think every stupid thought that comes into our head. We can reject it!

If our thinking is skewed and we are perpetually believing lies, we will consistently end up in emotional ditches.

Skewed Thinking

My own thinking is frequently skewed. I cannot trust it for one moment.

My thinking fluctuates with my emotions.

My emotions have no intelligence and must be examined and challenged. Can you identify your skewed thinking?

What thinking trap do I continually repeat?

Perhaps you have never known that you have the power within in you to discipline your own thinking and shape your own emotional wellness.

If the trauma isn't happening now, I can choose to not relive it!

Study character

Study the character traits of those around you.

This is not only humorous but can be empowering.

Negative Emotions

List every negative emotion you indulge and get rid of it.

Will you serve these fickle emotions or choose healthier responses?

Are these behaviors helping or hindering your recovery?

Do I need to have the last word?

Analyze every restless thought, every motive of your heart, and every word that comes from your mouth.

What words do I regret saying? Now write out an apology and share it with a trusted friend.

If every idle word returns to me, what words would I refuse to speak?

Am I prone to impulsive speech or idle gossip?

What boundary do I need to place on myself to stop this habit?

Based upon my words and actions today what seeds am I planting?

Love, joy, & peace or hatred, confusion & chaos.

Do I have to have the last word?

Old habits die hard. It takes practice.

Let someone else have the last word today.

Smile ... you have sown the seeds of peace.

Are you a sponge?

Can I rule my own disposition?

Do I soak up every oppressive, contentious mood around me and mirror it back at others?

If I have no control over my own moods, I am like a defenseless coward about to be overrun. Soon, whatever temperament is in front of me will be soaked up and become my own. If my co-worker is angry, now I am angry. If my partner is sad, now I am sad. I am just a wet sponge! Exhausting!

Necessary walls

I must build walls around my personality (heart) to be able to possess my own emotions or I will just be continually plundered.

Are you being plundered?

What work would you need to do to build an emotional wall to defend yourself against another's emotional instability?

I find I must harden my heart a little, and let others own their own stuff.

How are you purposefully repairing, building, and strengthening yourself?

Rise above my circumstances

1. Sit or position yourself to be emotionally above the situation.

2. Walk in love. Do not engage emotionally charged situations or manipulation.

3. Stand prepared with firm boundaries, patience, and kindness.

4. Be slow to make decisions. Slow to speak.

5. Do not get sucked into emotionally charged issues.

Conclusion

The journey of recovery for an enabler is not for cowards. It is not for those who enjoy playing the victim. It is not for those who love to control with emotional manipulation. Recovery from enabling is for those who are tired of torment and will do the work. Recovering Enablers pay a price for peace, safety, and stability in their lives.

An enabler who recovers is far more likely to have a loved one who sees the error of his way and chooses to do the work of recovery from their addictive behaviors also. An Enabler's recovery process, if actively pursued, with a strong counselor, friend or support group and will take 2-3 years.

Will we still have emotions? Oh yes, definitely! We will feel our emotions intensely for only minutes and then release them. These emotions will signal us to observe our motives and the motives of other people through their words and actions. **Emotions will not rule us and ruin our lives. The emotions will be signs and symptoms to discover the deeper root of what needs mastered in our lives.** We will no longer entertain emotional upheaval, fall prey to emotional manipulation or be dominated and destroyed by abuse (past or present). Mastering our emotions and using them to discover ourselves will give us power to enjoy each day!

The journey of recovery for an enabler is not for the fainthearted, as it is a journey of a thousand tears.

APPENDIX A

DETACHMENT: AN ENABLER'S SURVIVAL SKILL QUICK GUIDE

Healthy love does not fear letting go; sick love manipulates and controls consequences for irresponsible behavior which causes more dependency and prolongs suffering.

#1 Detachment is not cold, withdrawn, or isolated, but a decision to do what is best for myself first. It is a healthy boundary of knowing where my responsibility begins and where it ends. It is a healthy separation from toxic relationships and a healthy connectedness with others.

#2 Detachment is not caring less but caring more for my emotional stability. In this step, I need to understand my level of enmeshment. **Enmeshment is being entangled or wrapped up in someone else so much that I have lost my identity and have no peace.**

#3 Detachment is understanding my emotional stability is not dependent on another person or their sobriety.

#4 Detachment respects the boundaries of others to make their own choices and to have their own consequences.

#5 Detachment means "minding my own business". I will then have the energy to address my issues and be positioned with others who can mentor, encourage and hold me accountable.

#6 Detachment means forgiveness. This can empower me to seek and search for ways to detach and "let go" of my past and move forward with my life.

#7 Detachment means thinking differently. I can identify the thoughts I think about myself. Whose voice is in my head rejecting or controlling me?

#8 Detachment means if I see a tornado coming, I can hide in the cellar. I can find ways to disentangle my codependent, enabling behaviors from people who systematically control and manipulate me to finance their irresponsible behaviors. I can withdraw from those who are disorderly and understand it is not my responsibility to feed able bodied adults who refuse to work or squander resources.

#9 Detachment means to help bear another person's crisis, but to let him carry his own personal load. A crisis is an accident, injury, severe illness, or natural disaster. A personal load is paying my own utilities, car insurance, car payments, gas and food. I am not talking about the fiscally responsible poor, ill or sober homeless.

#10 Detachment means to allow myself to learn from my mistakes. This does not mean I will brood, beat myself up or turn to destructive behaviors. It is an honest evaluation of my actions and their outcomes. Then, I can pursue a plan to make my future look different from my past.

#11 Detachment means emotionally separating myself from my problem. This is simple, but not easy. Immaturity soaks up the emotions around me and mirrors them back. As I mature emotionally, I can feel my own emotions. I can change the things I can and release the things I cannot change and purpose to enjoy my day.

#12 Detachment means I can let go of another person's problem, choose to let them mature, and become stronger by allowing them to find their own solutions. Detachment is not abandonment, but a healthy love for myself and others. I can make decisions without fear or emotional manipulation. This includes gradual separation and launching of adult children into independent living. If I coddle adult children, it is more likely they will have a life of suffering and dependency.

The decisions I make will be rational, thought out and purposeful. I will not be an emotional puppet or a soft target for the addicted extortionist. I can guard myself from abuse with strong boundaries. I will acknowledge my addictive behaviors, including my behavior of rescuing and enabling. I will search for the root of my problems: a past wound, unmet need, guilt, a desire to keep my loved one from experiencing pain, or public embarrassment. Perhaps it is the misery of the consequences of defective choices, which will propel my loved one into recovery. In recovery, we can both encounter others to encourage, support us and find lasting peace. **The spiraling financial consequences, mental anguish, emotional chaos, and physical drain of enabling begs the voice of detachment to ensure self-preservation precisely as an Artic Expeditioner would strategically plans for his survival.**

Develop a back bone and demand progressive recovery!

APPENDIX B

ANGIE'S SNIPPETS OF WISDOM

Highlight the ones you like.

Chapter 1

1) Enablers are addicted to their loved one with SUD and need to work a recovery plan.

2) Detachment allows decision making to be based upon what is right for me.

3) My decisions are not based on manipulation.

4) Acceptance leads to peace.

5) The way to recover my loved one from this bondage is to recover myself first.

6) It is impossible to cure addiction issues with money.

7) The enabler is powerless to change another and must let go of the responsibility to do so.

8) The enabler must leave the decision of recovery in the hands of their loved one's hands.

9) Consequences can become a catalyst for change.

10) Enablers do not need to stay on the path of destruction with their loved one's with SUD.

11) Over-responsibility fosters our loved one's under-responsibility.

12) Rescuing your loved one from consequences assures the need for more destructive consequences.

13) The road of an enabler is mental torment and despair.

Chapter 2

14) When I disengage from toxic relationships, I will be the enemy.

15) Anxiety levels match the level of physical, emotional, and financial involvement in lunacy.

16) Only a person with SUD can choose to change themselves.

17) I need to protect my identity, or it could be stolen as payback.

18) Co-enablers cannot see their own issues but focus on the person with SUD as the main problem.

19) The primary enabler is obsessed with their loved one.

20) If the primary enabler is providing for the person with SUD, don't provide for them.

21) If I choose to live with a primary enabler and/or person with SUD, it will be a war zone.

22) There is no recovery if there is no accountability for the person with SUD or enabler.

23) These are painful relationships to be in or to watch from a distance.

Chapter 3

24) Self-pity consumes a lot of energy.

25) The imbalance of undisciplined thinking and exaggerated immature emotions results in self-destructive behaviors.

26) Persons with SUD and enablers suffer from an identity crisis.

27) Addictions make relationships and home environments unstable.

28) Instability diverts my attention from the root issues and fuels perpetual suffering.

29) Recovery is hard work!

Chapter 4

30) Only I can reshape my future to look different than my past.

Chapter 5

31) Recovering myself from a wounded heart, is a simple shift in my thinking.

32) Wounds keep me emotionally unstable and immature.

33) Facts give me mental thinking direction.

34) I can learn to be a safe person for myself.

35) Negative talk from myself or others hits the "sabotage" button.

36) When I recognize dysfunctional coping skills, I can stop and make healthier choices.

37) Unnecessary harshness from me causes more bitter responses from others.

38) Where negativity has been planted, I can expect thorny branches and rotten fruit.

Chapter 6

39) Foolish emotions, if indulged, take over my life.

40) Be patient with myself.

41) It takes time to conquer poor habits of undisciplined thinking.

42) I do not take a wound inside of myself but use it as a springboard for growth.

43) Negativity manifests itself in my life as anxiety and fear.

44) If I am currently being abused, it is not time to forgive.

45) Negative statements are a quick slide to destructive thinking.

46) Stay in the present and enjoy every precious moment.

47) Do not ruminate in the past or stress over the future.

48) Do not go back and ask for forgiveness when it would set you up for more abuse.

49) Do not assume outcomes of someone else's poor choices.

50) Do not go back to repent when it would open old wounds or make things worse.

51) Some people are not safe, and an accountability partner can help me identify them.

52) It is my responsibility to stop the abuse!

53) Just because nonsense entered my head does not mean I have to entertain it. There is no way to solve the unsolvable.

54) Negative rumination robs me of today!

55) Letting go is a developmental emotional maturity skill.

56) Individuals with SUD can be master extortionist.

57) Love one's with SUD and enablers are master manipulators.

58) A crazy maker will destroy the relationship and make it my fault.

59) I cannot recover until I am ready to assume full responsibility for my actions.

Chapter 7

60) True recovery plan for lasting change.

61) Bullies make outrageous demands.

62) Repentance never gives someone the upper hand to manipulate me...again.

63) Any plan to assist a loved one with SUD is conditional on them working a recovery plan.

64) Develop a backbone and demand progressive recovery!

65) Expect progress not perfection.

66) Whatever the hardest thing for me to do, is probably the best.

67) Cash usurps a loved one with SUD or primary enabler's willpower and alters healthy decision-making.

68) Think of cash as a cattle prod to drive loved one's with SUD to the slaughter.

69) My loved one's problems are not my problems.

Chapter 8

70) If I do not know what to do, I get counsel.

71) If I still do not know what to do, I wait and am not impulsive.

72) I can stop controlling circumstances and outcomes in the lives of other adults.

73) I can learn to say "no" without fear or anxiety.

74) Some things are broken, and it is ok.

75) Conflict cannot be resolved with one in active enabling or addictions.

76) Forgiveness gives me the power to release the pain and move forward.

77) Being ruled by my emotions means my day will certainly be stressful.

78) Distance myself from the unteachable.

79) Freedom to say "no" without repercussions makes a safe relationship.

80) Withdraw from those who are undisciplined.

81) Mind my own business. Do not pry or meddle.

82) Be quiet and busy taking care of my own responsibilities.

83) Do not associate with anyone who is irresponsible.

Chapter 9

84) Do not coddle irresponsibility and expect a responsible outcome.

85) Angry words do not bring healing.

86) Get out of the way and stop rescuing!

87) Each rescue is only a temporary fix.

88) If I become financially destitute, I will more likely be abused.

89) Any addictive path leads to loss and destruction.

90) Poor boundaries are like quicksand.

91) Every time I give a loved one with SUD cash, I have placed another nail in his coffin.

92) It is intense suffering to watch a loved one suffer.

93) There is a steep price to pay to give a loved one with SUD privileges he has not earned and has previously abused.

94) If I am a poor example, I can expect it exaggerated and mirrored back at me.

95) Individuals in recovery need to earn trust: enablers and loved one's with SUD.

Chapter 10

96) People in toxic relationships give power away to gain power and control over another.

97) If I keep hooking into the same type of dysfunctional people, I have lost my identity.

98) Enablers have not learned to trust others to find their own way.

99) Enablers have forgotten how to exercise their intuition.

100) Enablers do not know how to trust themselves.

100) Toxic people lack disciplined thinking.

101) If I am dating a person who dominates my thinking...I should run!

102) A ranting, negative person uses anger to self-medicate. The rage releases pent up emotions.

103) An individual with SUD divides me from my other loved ones to gain power over me.

104) Walking on eggshells to keep the peace is misery. There is never any real peace.

105) Name calling is the abuser's signature card.

106) Blaming and playing the victim is the game of a person with SUD.

107) An enabler is a master excuse maker.

108) Stop making excuses for poor behavior and set up standards for relationships.

109) Rescuing keeps others from experiencing the ramification of their choices.

110) Persons with SUD intentionally usurp my decision-making skills with emotional manipulation.

Chapter 11

111) Healthy relationships are intentional.

112) If I am not free to say "no", I will never be free to say "yes".

113) Healthy relationships need to ebb and flow and enjoy unity and separateness.

114) No relationship is healthy without the ability to be an individual with my own personality.

115) There is no safe relationship without trust.

116) Serving one another without expectations brings great joy.

117) It is a treasure to have someone in my life who cares about how I think and feel.

118) Bitterness can fester like annoying splinters.

119) Secrets in healthy loving relationships are surprises for holidays or gifts.

120) The consequences of hiding and lying is a pervasive feeling of loneliness.

Chapter 12

121) It is irresponsible to make a loved one dependent upon me for deliverance from poor choices.

122) Leave them in jail! Prison is better than the grave.

123) I must diligently protect my heart from the confusion and manipulation of others.

124) Mind my own business!

125) The purpose of distance is to bring peace and allow perspective.

126) When you get free from enabling, stand steadfast and do not be entangled again with it.

127) Enabling makes me captive in the bondage of confusion.

128) Do not feed the bears!

129) An expert manipulator can control my emotions and thinking.

130) Reject manipulation and stubbornness!

Chapter 13

131) Do not pay bail! Whatever I do, I am not to co-sign for them.

132) Confrontation (with patience and kindness) can be healthy!

133) I can practice patience and kindness with firm and strong boundaries.

134) It is necessary to address the manipulation within my own heart.

135) Deal with all my emotions before correcting or confronting another.

136) Get control over exaggerated emotions.

137) Others can be mirrors of my error.

138) Do not judge another.

139) Correct the stubborn and do not correct the stubborn and know the difference of when to speak or not to speak.

140) Don't waste my breath with a double-talking, backstabbing manipulator.

141) A sincere person can hear me.

142) If a person will not receive correction, wait for suffering consequences to come and they may be ready.

143) Opportunities for teaching is good when a person is frustrated and cannot figure out what to do.

144) Do not listen to gossip or slander. Do not be a gossip or slanderer.

145) Do not stay in close fellowship with a person who can be unpredictable or volatile.

146) Do not get dragged into someone else's problems.

147) Do not get in the middle of someone else's fight.

148) Do not argue with anger. If emotions are high. Walk away!

149) Do not be a busybody.

Chapter 14

150) Do not give another enough control to rob me of my joy.

151) Deceivers corrupt my mind from the simple life of love.

152) There is a cheater who can beguile me with a myriad of enchantments.

153) Manipulators can mimic respectable citizens.

154) Manipulators play enabler and co-enablers against each other.

155) Cut off any emotional manipulation.

156) Do not add to suffering by denying that anything is wrong.

157) Do not think I am wise and can solve perpetual problems of another.

158) Do not give others emotional control over me.

159) Do not give into fear.

160) Do not give manipulators control.

161) Do not allow a thief in your home.

162) Do not let down my guard with someone who has previously attacked me.

163) Do not feel sorry for people who receive consequences for poor choices.

164) Do not steal for anyone.

165) Do not leave children with immature, selfish caregivers.

166) Do not coddle adult children and allow them to wander on a path to nowhere!

167) Do not do anything for a loved one that responsible adults could/should do for themselves.

168) Acceptance of the right of another to make their own decisions and suffer their own consequences of their poor choices will give me back my life.

169) A "leg-up" for responsible young adults, or the working poor is one thing, enabling a perpetual pattern of addiction or irresponsibility is another.

170) Manipulation is rebellion and is the pathway to destruction.

171) Protect my heart from all stupidity.

172) Make decisions with my intellect and not my emotions.

173) Saving another is a noble thing. Sinking in their quicksand is not.

174) Do not mess with people who are temperamental.

Chapter 15

175) Undisciplined thinking makes me grumpy. Take charge of what I think and feel.

176) I can stay in the present moment and enjoy my day.

177) Recognize obsessive thinking and stop it.

Chapter 16

178) True love repents often.

179) Trust others to find their own path.

180) If I want mature devoted love, I must be whole enough to receive it.

Chapter 17

181) If I clean up my compulsive thinking and impulsive responses, I can find emotional stability.

182) Self-control over my speech and thoughts can establish me as an impenetrable fortress.

183) Meditation is like a mental shelter to withstand any storm.

184) Developing patience and self-control in no way makes me a doormat!

185) Maturity gives me the strength and courage to go to higher emotional ground.

186) Grumbling breeds an environment of discontent that is stressful to endure and drains my energy.

187) Be emotionally mature enough to stay out of the way of drama.

188) Do not usurp the growth experience of another.

189) Show no emotions with emotional manipulators.

190) Negative emotional games have temporary pretend power, but end in confusion and brokenness.

191) Patient, firm, kind, loving response gives me stability and self-control.

192) As I practice emotional stability, I can enjoy my life.

193) Negative emotions beget negative emotions; like dog begets dog.

194) Negative emotions, if indulged, are destructive.

195) A dependable person is likely to be a solid citizen with emotional stability.

196) A peaceful home does not just happen.

197) A peaceful home takes practice and responding to life's struggles by growing and maturing.

198) Serving persons with substance use disorder or abusive behaviors will not bring gratification.

199) A quiet and patient attitude will honor myself and others.

200) There is never an excuse to be unkind. Very firm, but patient and kind.

201) Practicing manners and common courtesies at home will provide stability and peace.

Chapter 18

202) There needs to be a decision to stop the anxiety, not to solve the problem.

203) Some of my problems are unsolvable and only acceptance leads to peace.

204) Stop the roller coaster and let me off.

205) Anxiety is a STOP sign to slow down and process life.

206) Purpose to live in the present moment and enjoy it.

207) Reject the thoughts that do not serve me well.

208) It should be normal to go to support group meetings or professional counseling when I cannot stop my anxiety.

209) Don't let fear hold me back from finding recovery.

210) Recognizing anxiety and admitting I need help is the biggest step in recovery.

211) Toxic people refuse boundaries.

212) People who refuse my boundaries are unsafe.

213) If I stay in a toxic relationship, I will lose my identity.

214) Manipulators play the victim.

215) When I recognize abuse, anger is common.

216) Let anger empower you to establish healthy boundaries and escape toxic relationships.

217) Be intentional to refuse anxiety and pursue peace.

218) I can throw out disrespectful, contemptuous people who refuse to respect my boundaries.

219) Turn every anxious thought into a grateful one.

220) Let peace reign in my heart.

221) What I believe about a situation is powerful.

222) What I say to myself about a circumstance is powerful.

223) Do not elevate my emotions to the level of truth. They are just emotions.

224) Anxiety is a self-induced form of suffering. It is within my power to stop it!

225) Place the responsibility of another adult's problems firmly upon their shoulders.

226) Do not rob others of the chance to mature, grow and experience victory in overcoming the burdens of poor decision making.

227) Rise up and claim the peace that is mine.

228) Recognize the seducing emotions that lure me down the rabbit hole of stress.

229) Denounce anxious, worrisome, and fearful thoughts.

230) Denial is a seductress that lures you with a promise and leaves you empty.

231) The key to unlock anxiety is courage! Courage to face life as it comes!

232) Anxiety, worry, and fear is me trying to control the wind.

233) A mental gym strengthens my correct reasoning and rids me of my flabby thinking.

234) Emotions will either rule me or I will rule them.

235) Emotions can build fortresses of false thinking and outright lies in my head.

236) Building my own identity gives me confidence to trust my decisions.

237) Focus on learning healthy coping skills and not on anxiety.

238) Embrace diligent, persistent, patient, steadfast character skills to produce stability.

239) Be faithful to care for my own needs first.

240) Occasionally, isolation can be a short-term antidote to help me process things irritating me.

241) Long-term isolation will leave me empty and lonely.

242) Isolation can keep me stuck in my head with no one to refute my irrational thinking.

243) Exaggerated minor irritations may be because of loss of control in other areas of life.

244) Accepting life with all its irritations brings peace.

245) Consider suffering a part of life and find benefits in it.

246) Practice flexibility and allow fluctuating circumstances to mold me into a better person.

247) Let each irritation become an opportunity to hold onto my peace.

248) Entertaining anxiety, worry or fear is a magnet for attracting more trouble.

249) Pressed down, shaken down, running over... whatever I give, I receive.

250) I have permission to laugh, smile and enjoy a lovely day.

251) This is a new day, let me find joy in it.

Chapter 19

252) Detach in love without fear.

253) Most people do not change without suffering.

254) Detachment brings peace.

255) Detachment is finding my healthy identity.

256) Almost every individual with addictive behaviors has an enabler who is also sick.

257) People caught in an addiction trap need more help than an enabler can give them.

258) Detachment respects the boundaries of others to make their own choices and to have their own consequences.

259) Detachment means, "minding my own business".

260) Detachment means forgiveness.

261) Detachment means thinking differently.

262) Courage is the secret to overcoming enabling behaviors.

263) Detachment means to get out of the whirlwind.

264) Make no friendship with stupidity.

265) Withdraw yourself from the confusion and disorder.

266) Do not engage an angry person until they have control over their emotions.

267) My sanity is too important to indulge immature emotions and behaviors.

268) Detachment means to bear another person's crisis, but to let him carry his own personal load.

269) If I am over-responsible, it will allow others to be under-responsible.

270) Detachment means to allow myself to learn from my mistakes.

271) Brokenness is a death of my expectations and the acceptance of the inability to change others.

272) Detachment means emotionally separating myself from the problem.

273) Coddling leads to a life of suffering and dependency.

274) Detachment means I can enjoy my day.

275) If I am dead (detached) to my emotions, I cannot be manipulated emotionally.

276) A calloused heart is stuck in pain, refuses change, and stays in a vicious cycle.

277) Learn to find the good in great times of sorrow.

278) Today, I can practice quietness inside and pursue contentment.

Chapter 20

279) Reject nonsense.

280) Deceitfulness can be so convincing when I believe the lies.

281) Do not let those in rebellion trap me emotionally or financially.

282) If I am trying to please unpleasable people, I have forgotten to be true to myself.

283) Those that use perversion of truth are masters at manipulation.

284) I cannot find balance in chaos. Turn off the chaos. Get alone. Get quiet.

285) My courage to change can give hope to another who needs to change.

286) Stand steadfast in freedom. Do not go back to the cycle of enabling.

287) Make others earn the right to be trusted.

288) If I sow to the wind, I will reap the whirlwind.

289) Hold my head high and speak no dirty words.

Chapter 21

290) Some people are in love with the idea of being in love, but not with me.

291) Lust can feel like true love.

292) Obsession can feel like devotion.

293) It does not matter, if the devourer rages or laughs, there is no peace.

294) A romantic relationship with a devourer can never match the fantasy and needs to be destroyed.

295) Be leery of anyone who consistently plays the victim.

296) A warped view of love is dominance and control.

297) A person with a divided heart and soul cannot love me.

298) Doublemindedness makes me unstable in all my ways.

299) Intense lust can be a sister to explosive anger.

300) Intense lust creates dysfunctional relationships.

301) Passive/aggressive behaviors keep me imbalanced.

302) Relationship failures repeat themselves if not explored and resolved.

303) Real relationships are not fairytales, they are work.

304) Detaching from my emotions can stop the manipulation and dominance over me.

305) Healthy boundaries are often met with the other person ending the relationship.

306) Recovery from enabling is work.

307) I can only control myself.

308) Attempting to control another will drive me crazy.

309) A crisis can be used to start the recovery process.

310) If I want my future to look different from the past, I must plan to change.

311) If I stay in an addictive relationship pattern, I will not like who I become.

312) Addictions never bring health or healing.

Chapter 22

313) Talk is cheap. Action speak volumes.

314) When it comes to recovery, do not expect perfection but do require progress.

315) Rescuing another from consequences to their poor choices is destructive.

316) Do not tolerate anger or manipulation.

317) Have courage and trust others to find their own path in life.

Chapter 23

318) Do not try to bear sorrow alone.

319) When my mental facilities are clear, I can choose a different path in life.

320) If I have tried to help someone caught in addictive behaviors for a decade, they are not doing the work of recovery.

321) I can expect to be an enemy when I choose to stop enabling.

322) Grieve and let go, grieve, and let go, grieve and let go.

323) Harden my heart towards an irresponsible person to protect myself.

324) Guard my heart from insanity.

325) If I grieve too long, I can stop and redirect my focus. Grieve in small bites at a time.

326) I can't cry a river for a decade, I will lose my own life.

327) Enabling is a self-induced suffering.

328) I am powerless over another person's addictive behaviors.

Chapter 24

329) Do not attempt to control the uncontrollable.

330) Identify a safe person today.

331) Do not let anxiety be my companion.

332) Recognize lies that set up mental strongholds that bind me in chains.

333) Anxiety shrouds me in darkness and robs me of healthy relationships.

334) Anxiety sets me on a path of loneliness and depression.

335) Anxiety dominates and controls. Do not entertain it.

336) Recognize repeating patterns of dysfunctional relationships.

337) It takes emotional maturity to choose healthy relationships.

338) Quiet meditative reflection leads to peace.

339) Anxiety is on the side of the enemy! Refuse it!

340) Seek pure love with the fierceness of a warrior.

341) Claim peace that is greater than my circumstances.

342) A purposeful walk of love and peace is not passive.

343) I choose mental soundness.

344) I can sit and observe the burdens of life with contentment.

345) Letting go of what I cannot change brings mental clarity of purpose.

346) Let nothing hinder me from experiencing a quiet and trusting heart.

347) Joy is my birthright.

348) Peace is my inheritance.

349) In quietness and confidence, I can find my strength.

350) I give myself permission to enjoy my day.

351) Do not let peace hide behind my problem or under my bed.

352) Chase after peace.

353) Be quiet.

354) Reject all chaos.

355) Skewed thinking lands me in an emotional ditch.

356) Do not trust exaggerated emotions.

357) I have the power to discipline my own thinking and shape my emotional wellness.

358) Do not choose to relive trauma.

359) Fickle emotions hinder me from making healthy choices.

360) Idle words return to me.

361) Old habits die hard. Practice patience with myself.

362) Recognize faintheartedness and replace it with courage.

363) Rule my own disposition by refusing mood swings and broodiness.

364) Position myself above my circumstances.

365) Rise above my circumstances.

REFERENCES

Alcoholics Anonymous. (1938). Akron, OH: Alcoholics Anonymous.

Dictionary by Merriam-Webster: America's most-trusted online dictionary. (n.d.). Retrieved from https://www.merrriam-webster.com/

How Al-Anon works for families and friends of alcoholics. (2008). Virginia Beach, VA: Al-Anon Family Group Headquarters.

Kubler-Ross, E. (1985). *On death and dying*. Enfield, N.S.W.: Royal Blind Society.

AUTHOR'S BIOGRAPHIES

Angie G. Meadows graduated from St. Mary's School of Nursing as a Registered Nurse, Marshall University with a Bachelor's in Nursing and Ohio State University with a Master's in Nursing. She has worked at multiple hospitals in multiple capacities. Angie is a keen observer of human behaviors as she has dealt with enablers and those with SUD over the years. She is currently a wife, mother, speaker, and writer. Her favorite past time is quilting.

Dr Perry Meadows graduated from Marshall University with a Bachelor of Science in Chemistry, Master of Science in Biological Sciences, and Doctor of Medicine. Dr Meadows completed his internship and residency at Marshall University School of Medicine in Family Practice and is a Fellow of the American Academy of Family Physicians. Dr Meadows also received his Juris Doctor from Salmon P. Chase College of Law, Northern Kentucky University and M.B.A. from Regis University. Dr Meadows speaks on a local, regional, and national level on topics related to substance use disorder. He is active in working with various community organizations across Central Pennsylvania in issues related to behavioural health and substance use disorder. His favorite past time is photography.

Sarah J. Meadows graduated from Liberty University with a bachelor's degree in psychology. She has worked in the public-school system as a Therapeutic Day Treatment Counsellor. She is currently pursuing a master's degree in Clinical Mental Health Counselling. Sarah enjoys her friends and her beloved corgi.

OTHER RESOURCES BY THE AUTHORS

An Enabler's Journey: A Christian Perspective ISBN: 9781732810211

https://www.amazon.com/Enablers-Journey-Christian-Perspective-ebook/dp/B07KDK1L1F/ref=pd_sim_351_2/147-3762080-9342150?_encoding=UTF8&pd_rd_i=B07KDK1L1F&pd_rd_r=58dcb7aa-921e-4665-b6f0-ce42ced569ff&pd_rd_w=fau3o&pd_rd_wg=wWRbM&pf_rd_p=6f740e39-0c25-4380-8008-7a4156dab959&pf_rd_r=3W4KGCECXB8C6AVDAQJ0&psc=1&refRID=3W4KGCECXB8C6AVDAQJ0

This book is 290+ pages and 24 chapters. It is almost the same book as *A Thousand Tear: An Enabler's Journey* except it has a 100+ Scriptures to validate the principles for dealing with people in relationships.

Enabler's Journey Recovery Plan: Enabler's Journey Recovery Series: Book 1 ISBN: 9781732810228

https://www.amazon.com/Enablers-Journey-Recovery-Plan-Book-ebook/dp/B07NTND743/ref=sr_1_1?dchild=1&keywords=angie+g+meadows&qid=1590167957&s=books&sr=1-1

This is a 100+ page Book One of a recovery workbook series. It guides individuals and clients to understand enabling behaviors and evaluate their current participation in perpetuating a person with SUD's illness. The enabler will learn to recognize the cycle of enabling, entanglement, excuses and beliefs that handicap an enabler from recovery. It also coaches in the courage needed for detaching from destructive people and circumstances we cannot control. The book includes an enabler's recovery plan, accountability questionnaire, self-care program and a plan for identifying unhealthy and healthy coping strategies. It will also guide the recovering enabler to determine a level of safe involvement with a person with SUD and how to identify true and false recovery, rebuilt trust, and avoid the snare of another enabling relationship. It will help us recognize dysfunctional thinking and our false belief system that keeps us entangled. There are 5 chapters from the original *A Thousand Tears: An Enabler's Journey* book and 3 extra in-depth recovery chapters and many added self-evaluation charts. This is a beginner book or small group book for an Enablers. It is short and concise with lots of diagrams and easy to understand flow charts. It is a great beginner tool with lots of reflective questions for counsellors or small groups to use in guiding enablers to recovery.

Enabler's Journey Detachment: Enabler's Journey Recovery Series Book 2: ISBN: 9781732810235
https://www.amazon.com/Enablers-Journey-Detachment-Recovery-Book-ebook/dp/B07RQWP5YR/ref=sr_1_fkmr0_2?dchild=1&keywords=angie+g+meadows+detachment&qid=1590168176&s=digital-text&sr=1-2-fkmr0

This book empowers us to learn survival skills with 12 DETACHMENT PRINCIPLES. The spiralling financial consequences, mental anguish, emotional chaos, and physical drain of enabling begs the voice of detachment to ensure self-preservation. This book is a useful tool in dealing with Substance Use Disorder, or other individuals with abusive or irresponsible behaviors. It includes many self-assessment tools: Entitlement Evaluation, Empowerment Plan, Helpless Trap, Healthier Me, Healthy Speech Evaluation, Negative Emotional Triggers, Unmet Needs, Obsessive Thinking Traps, Forgiveness, Bitterness, Reconciliation, Holidays, Suffering, Power to Stop Enabling, Self-Talk, Rules for Survival, practical steps, reflective thinking and much, much more.

Angie G. Meadows, RN, MSN, Perry Meadows, MD., JD, Sarah J. Meadows, BS

.

www.ingramcontent.com/pod-product-compliance
Lightning Source LLC
LaVergne TN
LVHW011345080426
835511LV00005B/134

9 7 8 1 7 3 2 8 1 0 2 0 4